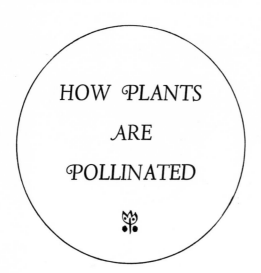

HOW PLANTS ARE POLLINATED

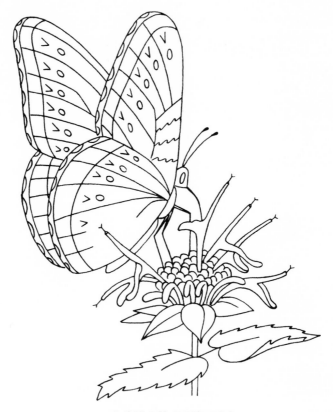

FRITILLARY BUTTERFLY
ON WILD BERGAMOT INFLORESCENCE

Joan Elma Rahn

HOW PLANTS ARE POLLINATED

ILLUSTRATED BY

Ginny Linville Winter

Atheneum · 1975 · New York

to Mary Adams Krauss

Library of Congress Cataloging in Publication Data
Rahn, Joan Elma,
How plants are pollinated.
SUMMARY: *Describes the many ways that flowers*
are pollinated and the pollinating agents that make the
differences in flowers possible.
1. Fertilization of plants—Juvenile literature.
[1. Fertilization of plants. 2. Flowers] I. Winter,
Ginny Linville. II. Title.
QK926.R33   582'.13'04166   75-9526
ISBN 0-689-30482-X

· Contents ·

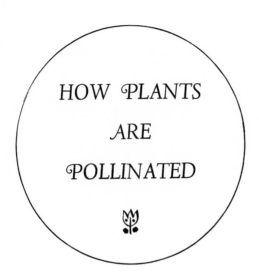

HOW PLANTS

ARE

POLLINATED

· Introduction ·

The ancient Babylonians and Hebrews had a special ceremony that they performed every year when the date palm trees bloomed. These ancient peoples knew that there are two types of date palm. One type produces no dates at all, but the flowers shed small grains called *pollen*. The pollen grains are so small that they look like powder or dust. The trees that produce pollen are male trees. The other type of date palm tree, the female tree, produces dates, but no pollen. However, dates form on the female trees only if their flowers receive pollen from the male trees. To ensure an abundant crop of dates, the ancient Babylonians and Hebrews cut flowering branches from the male trees and shook them over the flowers of the female trees.

The transfer of pollen from the male parts of a plant to the female parts of a plant is called *pollina-*

tion. All kinds of flowering plants are pollinated naturally—some by wind, some by insects or other animals, a few by water, and some by the plants themselves. They do not have to be pollinated artificially by people. Yet farmers and gardeners and other persons interested in plants should know something about the subject so that they do not do anything that will interfere with the pollination of the plants in their fields or gardens. Like the Babylonians and Hebrews, they also might want to do something that will improve pollination.

Actually, everyone should know something about pollination, for nearly all our food comes from plants that must be pollinated if they are to produce fruit and seeds, or from the animals that eat those plants. Of course, we could still have foods from plants that reproduce by underground parts—like potatoes or onions—and we would have many kinds of seafood. But without pollination, we could not have peaches, pears, strawberries, carrots, beets, cabbage, pumpkins, spinach, breakfast cereals, corn on the cob, macaroni and cheese, hamburgers on buns, hot dogs with mustard, scrambled eggs, fried chicken, apple pie, chocolate ice cream, or most of the other foods we eat. Neither would there be many trees, from which we get lumber to build homes, furniture, and other things, nor cotton plants, from the seeds of which at least some of our clothes are made.

Pollination is accomplished in different ways in different kinds of plants. The description of how it occurs in a particular plant is sometimes called its pollination story.

· Why Is Pollination · Important to Plants?

To understand pollination, you should first become familiar with the parts of a flower. If you can, get some chickweed plants in bloom and examine them for the parts described in the next paragraphs. Chickweed is a common weed in lawns and gardens, and probably no one will stop you from taking all you want. The flowers are very small, but you can recognize them easily because they look like little white stars with ten points. In fact, another name for chickweed is starwort. You should be able to find them in bloom from late spring to early autumn. If you have the opportunity to visit a greenhouse, you probably can get some chickweed in winter, too, for it often grows on the soil in flowerpots.

If you cannot find any chickweed plants in bloom, use the drawings on pages 8 to 12. You might also use any other type of fresh flower available to you, but remember that other kinds of flowers will not be exactly like the description that follows.

When examining flowers described in this book, you may find it helpful to use a magnifying glass or hand lens. This is not absolutely necessary, but it will make tiny flowers or small flower parts easier to see.

Flowers have four main parts: *sepals, petals, stamens,* and *pistils.*

The *sepals* of chickweed flowers—and of most other flowers as well—are green and look like leaves. Each chickweed flower has five sepals. They are the lowest parts of the flower. In a flower bud, the sepals are the outermost parts of the unopened flower, and they surround the other flower parts. Taken together, the sepals of a flower are called the *calyx.*

Just above the sepals are the *petals.* In most plants they are shaped like leaves but are some color other than green. Chickweed has five white petals in each flower. They are unusual petals because each one is so deeply notched that it almost looks like two. At first you think the flower has ten petals, but there are only five. Very few plants have petals notched as deeply as this. Taken together, the petals of a flower are called the *corolla.*

The calyx and the corolla together make up the *perianth* of the flower.

Above the petals are *stamens.* Most chickweed flowers have ten stamens, but there may be as few as three. The stamens are the male parts of the flower.

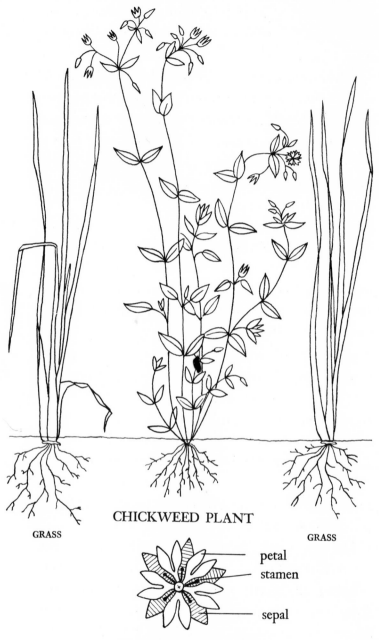

CHICKWEED PLANT

GRASS   GRASS

petal
stamen

sepal

CHICKWEED FLOWER

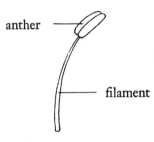

anther

filament

CHICKWEED STAMEN

Each stamen consists of two parts: a *filament* and an *anther*. The *filament* is a stalk. At the top of the filament is an *anther* in which the pollen grains are produced. Some of the anthers in your flower may be shedding pollen. Touch your finger lightly to one of the anthers. If some pollen comes off onto your finger, you will be able to feel how fine the pollen grains are. Although pollen looks like dust to you, the pollen grains of each species (or kind) of flowering plant have their own peculiar shape and markings, which can be seen with a microscope.

Each pollen grain consists of only two living cells: one is called a *tube cell*, the other a *generative cell*. If a pollen grain lands on the pistil of a flower, both cells play an important part in reproduction of the plant.

In the center of the chickweed flower is one *pistil*, which is the female part of the flower. The pistil has three parts: *ovary, styles,* and *stigmas.* The *ovary* is the lower, swollen portion of the pistil. Above are

HOW PLANTS ARE POLLINATED

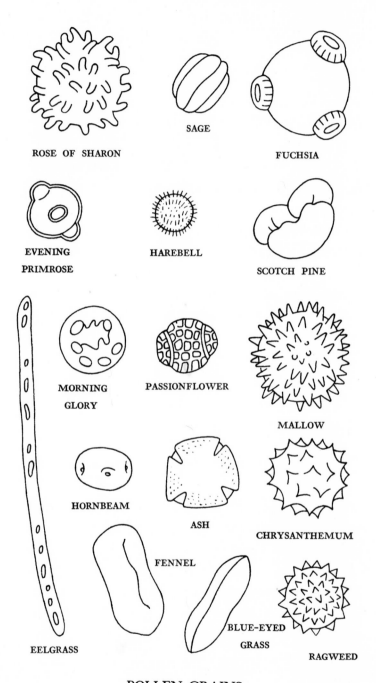

ROSE OF SHARON

SAGE

FUCHSIA

EVENING
PRIMROSE

HAREBELL

SCOTCH PINE

MORNING
GLORY

PASSIONFLOWER

MALLOW

HORNBEAM

ASH

CHRYSANTHEMUM

EELGRASS

FENNEL

BLUE-EYED
GRASS

RAGWEED

POLLEN GRAINS

three (or perhaps four or five) stalks; each of these is a *style*. At the tip of each style is a *stigma*.

With a sharp razor blade cut very carefully across an ovary. Inside you will see several very small, white objects called *ovules*. They are so small you probably will need a magnifying glass to see them well.

Inside each ovule is an *embryo sac;* it is called this because an *embryo*, or young plant, may develop within it if the pistil is pollinated. The embryo sac cannot be seen without the use of a microscope. It contains several cells. Two of them, the *egg cell* and the *central cell*, are important to the pollination story. But first, let us return to the pollen grains.

Although pollen might land on any part of a pistil, ordinarily only the pollen grains that land on a

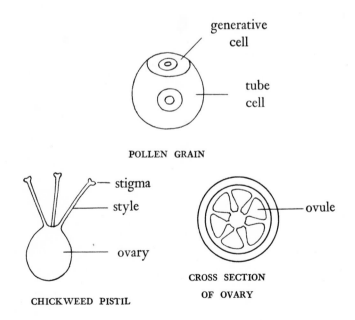

generative
cell

tube
cell

POLLEN GRAIN

stigma

style

ovary

CHICKWEED PISTIL

ovule

CROSS SECTION
OF OVARY

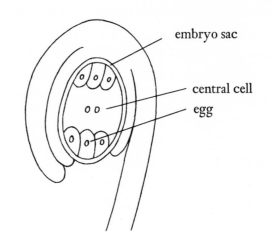

embryo sac

central cell

egg

OVULE

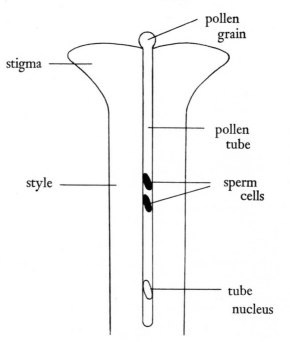

pollen grain

stigma

pollen tube

style

sperm cells

tube nucleus

POLLEN GRAIN
GROWING THROUGH STYLE

mature, or *receptive*, stigma begin to grow, or germinate. The tube cell forms a long tube called the *pollen tube*, which grows through the stigma and down through the style to an ovule in the ovary. The generative cell moves down the pollen tube, and while it moves it divides into two *sperm cells*. When the pollen tube reaches an ovule, the tip of the tube enters the embryo sac and bursts open. The two sperm cells move into the embryo sac, and one of them unites with the egg cell of the embryo sac. This uniting of the two cells is called *fertilization*. At the same time, the second sperm cell fertilizes the central cell of the embryo sac.

The fertilized egg grows into an embryo within the embryo sac. When this happens, the ovule begins to ripen into a *seed*. If the egg cell is not fertilized, no embryo forms, and the ovule ordinarily dies. In some plants, the fertilized central cell grows into a tissue called *endosperm*. This tissue stores food that the embryo will use if the seed is planted and the embryo grows into a seedling. In other plants, little or no endosperm forms, and the embryo stores all its own food. Some plants with endosperm in their seeds are dates, castor beans, onion, and the cereal grains, such as corn, wheat, rice, and oats. Some seeds with little or no endosperm are those of cucumbers, squash, beans, peas, sunflowers, and orchids.

When the ovules in an ovary ripen into seeds, the ovary ripens into a fruit. Most ovaries will not become fruits unless their ovules are ripening into seeds (bananas, pineapples, and a few other seedless fruits are exceptions). Thus pollination is important not only in the reproduction of flowering plants but in the production of food we eat. If pollination did not occur, no pollen grains would reach the stigmas, no pollen tubes would grow to the ovules, fertilization would not occur, no embryos would form, and no seeds or fruits would be produced.

· Recognizing · Flower Parts

Before considering the details of different types of pollination, you should become familiar with some variations in flowers and flower parts so that you can recognize them in different species of flowering plants. The sepals, petals, stamens, and pistils vary from species to species in sizes, shapes, colors, or arrangements.

Although most sepals are green and leaflike, a few flowers have sepals that are colored like the petals. Easter lilies, for instance, have three white sepals and three white petals, and in day lilies the sepals and petals are orange. In each case you can tell which is which because the sepals are to the outside of the petals. Sepals and petals that look very much alike are sometimes called *tepals* or just *perianth parts*.

Most petals are flat like leaves, but most of them are a different color from the leaves—usually white,

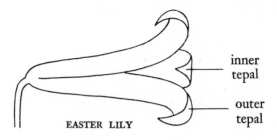

inner
tepal

outer
tepal

EASTER LILY

red, orange, yellow, blue, or violet. Some have several colors. As we shall see later, flowers pollinated by animals usually have large, brightly colored petals. All the petals of a flower need not be identical. In peas and beans, each flower has one large petal and four smaller ones arranged in two pairs. Orchids have one large petal called a *labellum*. Some flowers produce nectar that is stored in *spurs*, which are long sacs that are a part of one or more petals, or occasionally of sepals. Each petal of a columbine flower has its own spur, and a butter-and-eggs (toadflax) flower has one spur formed by several petals fused together.

Stamens have various sizes and shapes. The filaments may be short or long, wide or slender; most are cylindrical, but some are flat. Fine hairs cover the filaments of spiderwort and waterleaf.

One end of an anther may be attached to the filament, as in tulips, or the filament may be attached at the center of the anther, as in geraniums and Easter lilies. Many anthers, such as those of the geranium and tulip, have slits which open and through which the pollen grains are shed. Some anthers, like those of heather, barberry, and blueberry, shed pollen through pores rather than slits. In self-heal (heal-all), only one half of each anther is fertile and produces pollen grains; the other half is sterile and produces no pollen. In cannas, four of the five stamens are completely sterile, and they look so much like

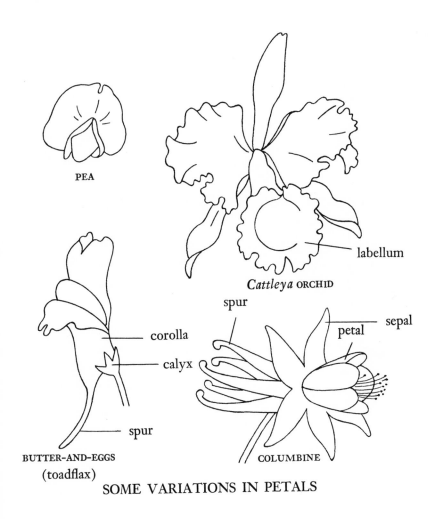

PEA

labellum

Cattleya ORCHID

spur

petal

sepal

corolla

calyx

spur

BUTTER-AND-EGGS
(toadflax)

COLUMBINE

SOME VARIATIONS IN PETALS

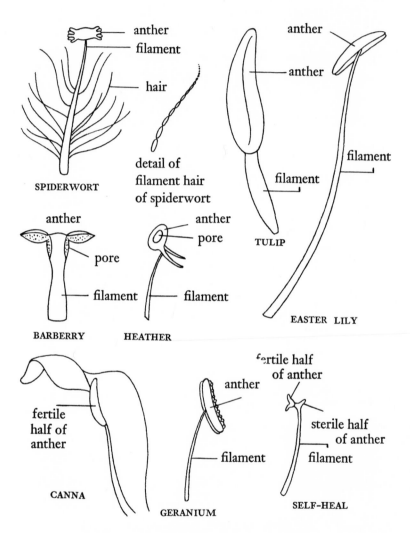

anther
filament

hair

detail of
filament hair
of spiderwort

SPIDERWORT

anther
anther

filament

filament

TULIP

anther
pore

anther
pore

filament
filament

BARBERRY   HEATHER

EASTER LILY

fertile half
of anther

anther

fertile
half of
anther

sterile half
of anther

filament

filament

CANNA

GERANIUM

SELF-HEAL

SOME VARIATIONS IN STAMENS

petals that they are easily mistaken for them. Half of the fifth stamen looks like half of a petal, and only the other half is fertile.

Pistils, too, come in different sizes and shapes. The ovary of the Easter lily pistil is longer and more slender than that of chickweed. It has one style even longer and more slender than the ovary, and there is a single stigma at the tip of the style. Some pistils, like those of chickweed, have several styles; others, such as those of tulip, poppy, May apple, and barberry, have no styles at all, and their stigmas are directly above their ovaries. May apple has one stigma, and bindweed two, rose of Sharon five. The stigma of Easter lily has three lobes. Grass flowers have branched stigmas; some branch so many times that they appear to be feathery. A little "skirt" surrounds the stigma of myrtle.

Most stigmas have some kind of adaptation that holds the pollen grains in place after they land there. The next time you see a lily in bloom, touch the stigma gently with the tip of your finger and notice how sticky it is. Once a pollen grain arrives on the stigma, it is not likely to fall off. The sticky material also contains a great deal of food that helps to nourish the pollen and its pollen tube as it grows down the long style to the ovary. The stigmas of rose of Sharon and hibiscus, on the other hand, are covered with short hairs. When the pollen grains land between the hairs, they become trapped.

Nearly all pistils have only one ovary; but the two

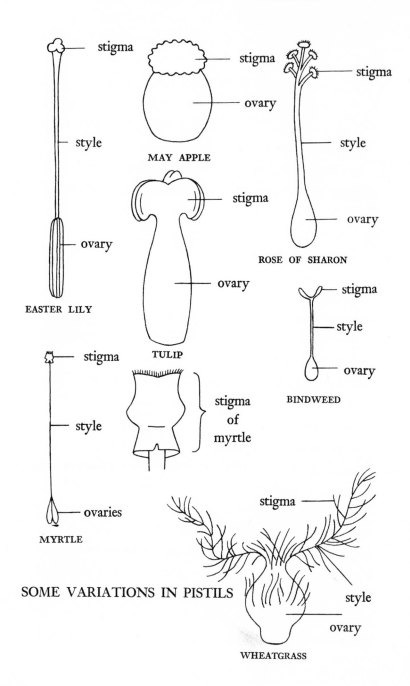

stigma

style

ovary

EASTER LILY

stigma

ovary

MAY APPLE

stigma

ovary

TULIP

stigma

style

stigma
of
myrtle

MYRTLE

stigma

style

ovary

ROSE OF SHARON

stigma

style

ovary

BINDWEED

SOME VARIATIONS IN PISTILS

stigma

style

ovary

WHEATGRASS

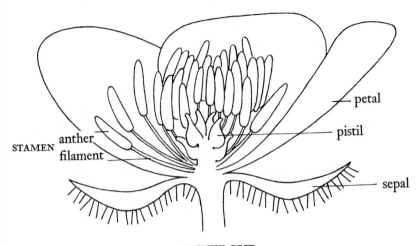

BUTTERCUP

pistils of myrtle, dogbane, and oleander have separate ovaries, which are joined at the top by a single style.

The parts of a flower are not always separate from each other, as they are in buttercups, for instance, where you can see distinctly each sepal, each petal, each stamen, and each pistil. In many plants, some parts are fused to each other.

The petals of morning glory flowers are fused into a funnel-shaped corolla. In snapdragon flowers, the petals are united into a tubular corolla open at one end (the dragon's mouth); it is only at the mouth of the tube that you can tell that there are five petals in the corolla—two in the upper lip and three in the lower. If you put your thumb on one side of a snapdragon flower and your forefinger on the other and squeeze gently, the mouth will open, and you can see the pistil and the stamens inside the corolla. The corolla tube of a phlox flower is ·very long and slender; on the other hand, heather and lily-of-the-valley have short, wide, urn-shaped corollas. In forsythia, the petals are fused near the base, so when you glance quickly at the flower you think it has four separate petals, but if you look more closely, you will see that the petals really are united.

In a few plants, the filaments of the stamens are fused to each other. They form a tube around the pistil, as they do in hibiscus, rose of Sharon, and lupine. In dandelions, the anthers are fused into a

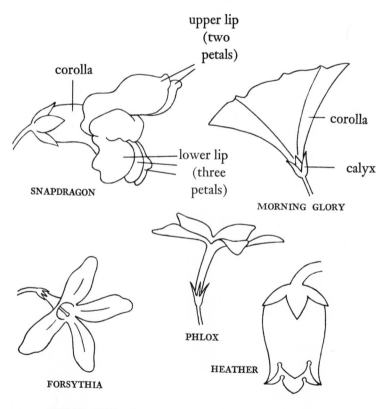

SOME COROLLAS WITH FUSED PETALS

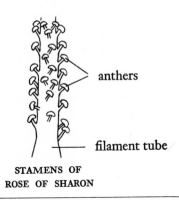

anthers

filament tube

STAMENS OF
ROSE OF SHARON

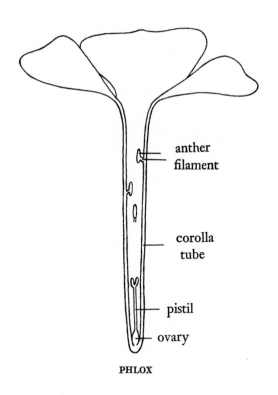

anther
filament

corolla
tube

pistil

ovary

PHLOX

tube around the single style, but the filaments are separate from each other.

Two different kinds of flower parts may be fused to each other, too. In phlox, primrose, and hyacinth, the filaments of the stamens are united to the corolla tube. The filaments seem to grow out of the corolla partway up the tube, but when you look closely, you usually can see that the filaments extend all the way to the bottom of the corolla. In orchids, the stamens and the pistil are fused so closely in the center of the flower that you can hardly tell them apart.

Sometimes you will have difficulty finding the ovary of a pistil. This may be because the bases of the sepals, petals, and stamens are all fused to each other and to the ovary. This makes it look as if the ovary is below the flower. Sometimes it helps to turn the flower upside down to locate the ovary. Such flowers are called *epigynous* because it looks as if the sepals, petals, and stamens are growing out of the top of the ovary. The prefix *epi* means *upon*, and *gyn* refers to something female, in this case, the ovary. Some epigynous flowers are those of the enchanter's nightshade, squash, cucumber, orchids, Queen Anne's lace, iris, gladiolus, bananas, blueberry, fuchsia, apple, pear, sunflower, dandelion, and many cactuses.

In a few plants, the fused bases of the sepals, petals, and stamens form a cup around the ovary, but the cup is separate from the ovary. Such flowers are called *perigynous* because it looks as if the sepals, petals, and stamens grow from the rim of the cup, which sur-

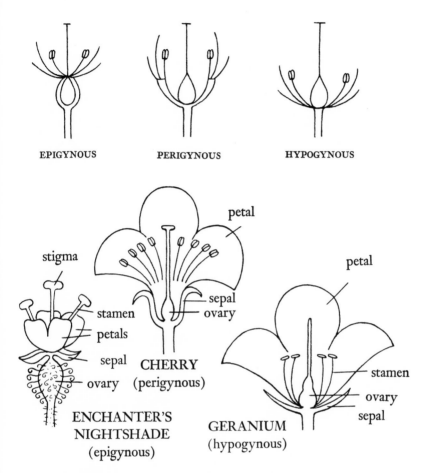

EPIGYNOUS   PERIGYNOUS   HYPOGYNOUS

petal

stigma

stamen

petals

sepal

ovary

ENCHANTER'S
NIGHTSHADE
(epigynous)

sepal
ovary

CHERRY
(perigynous)

petal

stamen

ovary

sepal

GERANIUM
(hypogynous)

rounds the ovary. The prefix *peri* means *around* or
surrounding. Some perigynous flowers are those of
cherry, plum, peach, rose, and some cactuses.

Flowers in which the bases of sepals, petals, and
stamens are not fused are called *hypogynous* because
those flower parts grow from below the ovary. The
prefix *hypo* means *below.* Some hypogynous flowers

are those of chickweed, buttercup, lilies, tulip, hibiscus, geranium, heather, mustards, phlox, and grasses.

The number of sepals, petals, stamens, and pistils varies from one species to another and sometimes even from flower to flower on the same plant. Most flowers have only a few of each kind of flower part—three, four, five, six, or perhaps a dozen or so—and you can count them easily. But other flowers have so many parts that it becomes difficult or at least tiresome to count them. The royal water lily has only 4 sepals but at least 50 petals, 150 stamens, and 30 pistils. Buttercup and strawberry flowers have only 5 sepals and 5 petals, but many more stamens and pistils. Some cactuses have a great many petals and stamens, but only 1 pistil.

Some flowers lack one or more of the four flower parts. Hepaticas and anemones, for instance, have no petals, but their sepals are colored like petals and look like petals. The tiny flowers of willow trees have neither sepals nor petals, but each flower has a hairy scale. Some plants, like willow, poplar, oak, corn, and the date palm, have two kinds of flower. One kind has stamens but no pistils; these are male, or *staminate*, flowers. The other kind has pistils but no stamens; they are female, or *pistillate*, flowers.

With this information and a little practice, you should be able to recognize the parts of most flowers when you see them. You may have difficulties with some varieties of garden flowers, especially those called "double-flowering." These varieties have been

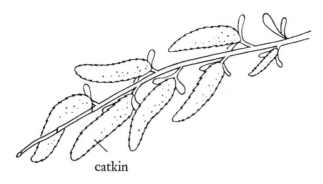

catkin

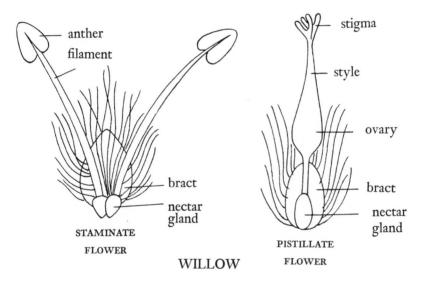

anther
filament

stigma

style

ovary

bract

nectar
gland

STAMINATE
FLOWER

bract

nectar
gland

PISTILLATE
FLOWER

WILLOW

cultivated for many generations because of their extra
petals. Most of these plants have poorly formed
stamens and pistils, and some have none at all. The
carnations you buy in a florist's shop are good examples. So are some ornamental fruit trees, like
double-flowering cherry and apple.

You must be careful, also, not to confuse an
inflorescence with a single flower. An inflorescence is

a group of flowers that grow close together on a stem. Sometimes the flowers of an inflorescence are so small and so close together that the inflorescence looks like just one flower. Break open the yellow head of a dandelion, and you will see that the head is an inflorescence composed of many yellow flowers. The lacy appearance of Queen Anne's lace (wild carrot) is due to the somewhat loose arrangement of small white flowers in a larger inflorescence (but the center flower is usually dark red). Sunflowers, milkweeds, Dutchman's-breeches and lilacs have flowers in inflorescences, too. The tiny flowers of willows are in staminate and pistillate inflorescences called *catkins;* they contain staminate and pistillate flowers respectively. The "paws" of pussy willows are staminate catkins, and their "fur" is the hairs on the scales.

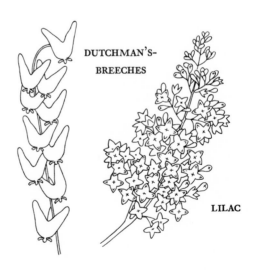

DUTCHMAN'S-
BREECHES

LILAC

· Cross-Pollination ·

A pollen grain in an anther must reach the stigma of a flower of the same species if that pollen grain is to bring about fertilization of an egg in an ovule. However, pollen grains have no power of movement. They cannot fly, swim, or crawl to a stigma. Something else must carry them there. Animals—especially insects—and wind are the most common pollinators. Only a few flowers are pollinated by water.

Self-pollination is the transfer of pollen grains from an anther to a stigma of the same flower or of another flower on the same plant. Most flowers set healthier and more numerous seeds if the pistils receive pollen grains from flowers of different plants (but of the same species); this is called *cross-pollination*. Most plants have some ways of preventing self-pollination or at least making it unlikely.

If some plants of a species have only staminate flowers and other plants have only pistillate flowers, self-pollination is impossible, for there are no pistils on the plants that produce the pollen. Such plants are called *dioecious* (pronounced die eé shus). This word comes from two Greek words; *di*, meaning two, and *oikos*, meaning house. Thus dioecious plants are those in which the staminate and pistillate flowers are in two different "houses," that is, on separate plants. Some dioecious plants are the box elder, the willows, and the poplars.

Plants that have separate staminate and pistillate flowers but have them on the same plant are called *monoecious* (mo neé shus); that is, both types of flower are in one "house." Some monoecious plants are begonia, butternut, walnut, oak, beech, birch, hazelnut, and corn.

On many monoecious plants, the staminate and pistillate flowers on any one plant bloom at different times. As a result, self-pollination is not likely. If you have a begonia plant in your home or garden, you have an opportunity to see this. When a begonia begins to bloom, the first flowers to appear are staminate; the pistillate flowers bloom later. These pistillate flowers may be pollinated from staminate flowers on another begonia plant that began to bloom later. On some butternut trees, all the pistillate flowers bloom first, then all the staminate flowers. On other butternut trees the staminate flowers bloom first, then the pistillate flowers. Whenever the stigmas on one

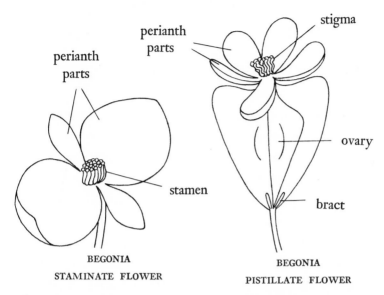

BEGONIA
STAMINATE FLOWER

BEGONIA
PISTILLATE FLOWER

butternut tree are receptive, another butternut tree is likely to be producing pollen. Actually, in plants with this arrangement, the times of blooming of staminate and pistillate flowers on a plant often overlap just a little, as you may discover if you watch a begonia plant closely. This allows both cross-pollination and self-pollination. If cross-pollination does not occur—perhaps because there is no other plant of the same species nearby—then at least some seed can be produced by self-pollination.

Most plants have both stamens and pistils in the same flower. Such flowers are *hermaphroditic*. This term, which means having both male and female parts, is derived from the names of a male character and a female character from Greek mythology—the god Hermes and the goddesss Aphrodite.

In some hermaphroditic flowers, self-pollination does not occur because the anthers shed pollen at one time and the stigmas are receptive at another time. Some avocado (alligator pear) plants have flowers in which the stigmas are receptive only in the morning and the anthers shed pollen only in the afternoon. Other avocado plants have flowers with anthers that shed pollen only in the morning and stigmas that are receptive only in the afternoon. In the morning, the second type of avocado plant may pollinate the first and in the afternoon, the first pollinate the second.

In many plants pollinated by animals, the stigma of a flower may be receptive at the same time the anthers are shedding pollen, but the positions of the stigma and anthers are such that the visiting animal first touches the stigma, then the anthers. In this way, if the animal has pollen from one flower on its body, some of this pollen may brush off onto the stigma of a second flower before the animal touches the anthers of that second flower. When the animal visits a third flower, it carries pollen from the second flower (and perhaps some from the first, too), and so pollinates that flower.

Of course, this does not necessarily prevent self-pollination. Animals often visit several flowers on the same plant before moving to another plant. Watch bees on a fruit tree in bloom, and you probably will see them visit many flowers on the same tree. However, occasionally some of them move from tree to tree, and this brings about cross-pollination.

In many plants, the pollen tube grows much faster if a pollen grain lands on a stigma of a different plant than if it arrives on a stigma of the plant from which it came. This is because some pistils produce substances that inhibit the growth of pollen tubes of pollen grains from the same plant. Then, if a flower is both self-pollinated and cross-pollinated, the pollen grains from other plants are much more likely to reach the ovules first.

Finally, in a few species, such as tomatoes and garden peas, self-pollination is the rule, and cross-pollination is rare. These plants produce abundant and healthy seeds without cross-pollination.

· Pollination ·
by Wind

In spring, about the time the first leaves begin to emerge from the buds on the trees, there also appear special short stems on some trees. These stems hang limply and sway with the gentlest breeze. Depending on the species of tree—and a little on your imagination—from the distance these stems look like limp strings or fat worms. When you look a little closer, you can see that each of them bears one or more very small flowers. Some trees with such tiny flowers dangling in the wind are: box elder, oaks, poplars (cottonwoods and aspens), walnut, and birch. All are pollinated by the wind, but each has somewhat different flowers in somewhat different arrangements.

To see what these flowers are like, we will look at two common American trees—box elder and oak—and at one important crop plant—corn—which is also wind-pollinated.

Box elder is a dioecious tree that grows as a weed throughout much of the United States. Young trees small enough that you can reach their flowers may often be found in vacant lots and along the edges of parks or farm fields where plants are allowed to grow wild. On the staminate plants, an inflorescence consists of several long, drooping stems, each with one staminate flower at the tip. If you examine one of these flowers, you will find it very simple. There are

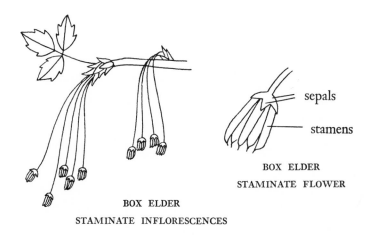

sepals

stamens

BOX ELDER
STAMINATE FLOWER

BOX ELDER
STAMINATE INFLORESCENCES

five sepals so small that you can barely see them without a magnifying glass. There are no petals. The five stamens have filaments so short that you cannot see them without taking the flower apart. The anthers, however, extend beyond the sepals and are readily visible.

On pistillate box elder trees, each inflorescence consists of a drooping, branched stem with one flower at the tip of each branch. The flowers lack petals and have tiny sepals like those of the staminate flowers. In the center of the flower is one pistil. The ovary is green and has two red wings, one on each side. The style is short but branches into two long, fuzzy stigmas. Like the staminate flowers, the pistillate flowers hang upside down.

Oak trees, too, are dioecious. They grow naturally over the eastern half of the United States and along

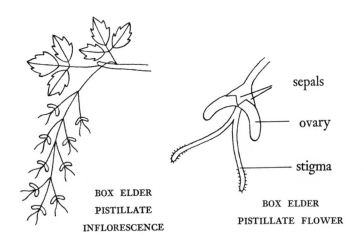

BOX ELDER
PISTILLATE
INFLORESCENCE

sepals

ovary

stigma

BOX ELDER
PISTILLATE FLOWER

the West Coast, but because they are such handsome trees, they often are planted elsewhere for ornamental purposes. The flowers and leaves appear about the same time in spring. The staminate flowers are easy enough to find. Short, drooping stems, each looking like a string with several knots in it, hang in clusters. If you look closely you will see that each "knot" is a staminate flower. It has several sepals (usually six),

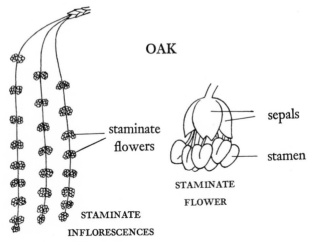

OAK

staminate
flowers

sepals

stamen

STAMINATE
FLOWER

STAMINATE
INFLORESCENCES

no petals, and several stamens (usually five or six). The anthers extend beyond the sepals, as they do in box elder.

The pistillate flowers of oak are not so easy to find. They are very small and occur alone or in groups of two or three. You must look along the twigs at the places where a new leaf is growing. At just this point you may find one or a few pistillate flowers. Of

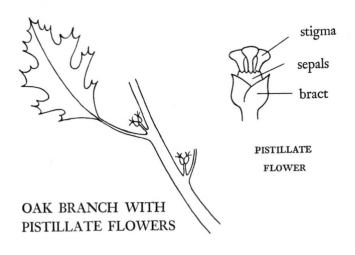

stigma

sepals

bract

PISTILLATE
FLOWER

OAK BRANCH WITH
PISTILLATE FLOWERS

course, not every leaf will have flowers near its base. Each flower has one small pistil surrounded by six tiny sepals and several small *bracts* (modified leaves), but these probably are too small for you to see easily even with a strong magnifying glass or hand lens. What you probably can just barely see are three styles and three stigmas that extend beyond the sepals and bracts.

Corn is one of the most important crop plants of the world, and more than half of it is raised in the United States—primarily in the Midwest. Corn does not grow wild, so you will find it growing only on farms or in vegetable gardens. Corn is monoecious. It flowers in midsummer after all its leaves have formed.

At the top of the corn plant is the staminate inflorescence called a tassel. It contains several branches bearing many staminate flowers. The perianth parts are small and pale green. Each flower has three stamens; their fine, slender filaments extend beyond the perianth parts and let the anthers tremble in the slightest breeze. Pollen comes out of two pores at the tips of the anthers and then is blown away by the breeze.

About the middle of the corn plant are one or two ears, each of which is a pistillate inflorescence. Several large green bracts called husks cover the entire inflorescence. If you were to peel these back at pollination time, you would find rows of pistillate flowers covering the ear. Each flower has only one pistil. The ovaries of all the pistils on the ear resemble

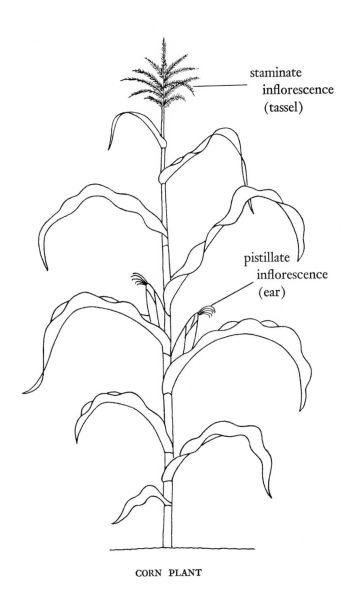

staminate
inflorescence
(tassel)

pistillate
inflorescence
(ear)

CORN PLANT

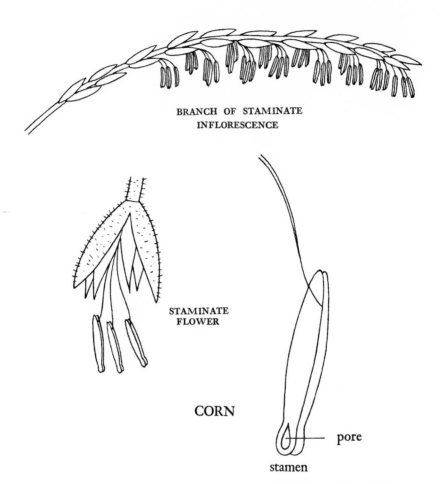

BRANCH OF STAMINATE
INFLORESCENCE

STAMINATE
FLOWER

CORN

pore

stamen

the kernels on an ear of sweet corn ready for eating—
and this is just what they will become a few weeks
after pollination. Perhaps the most remarkable thing
about a corn pistil is its style, which usually is at least
six inches long. The styles are the silks of the ear.
Each style has a slightly fuzzy appearance because of
its covering of fine hairs, each of which is a stigma.

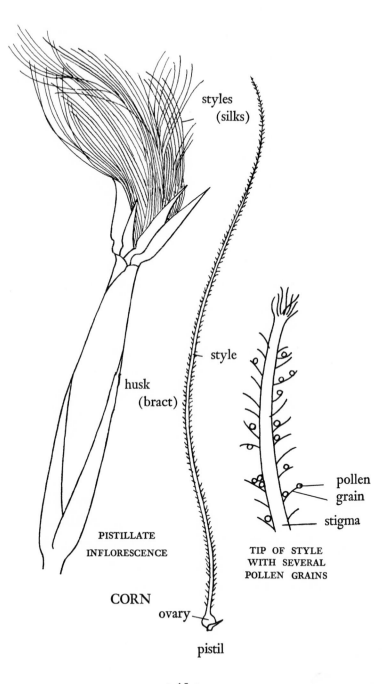

styles
(silks)

style

husk
(bract)

pollen
grain

stigma

PISTILLATE
INFLORESCENCE

TIP OF STYLE
WITH SEVERAL
POLLEN GRAINS

CORN

ovary

pistil

A flower has several perianth parts so small that they are difficult to see, for they are not even as tall as the ovary. The next time you have finished eating fresh corn on the cob, examine the cob before discarding it. Around each depression where a kernel has been, you can see these little perianth parts, for many of them remain there as you bite off the kernels (though a few may get between your teeth and annoy you for a while after dinner).

The flowers and inflorescences of box elder, oak, and corn all look different from each other. Yet they share certain similarities with each other and with other wind-pollinated plants as well. Although almost all wind-pollinated flowers are small and inconspicuous, their anthers and stigmas are freely exposed to the wind. The perianth parts are small and do not cover the anthers or the stigmas. The leaves do not interfere with the movement of pollen either. In box elder and oak, the leaves are still young and small at pollination time. In corn, the tassels stand above the highest leaves, and the silks are held well out from the stem in the large spaces between the leaves.

Pollen of wind-pollinated plants must be very fine and light, otherwise the wind could not carry it far. If you should be near a wind-pollinated plant at the time the anthers are open you might see pollen being blown away. On a calm day, jostle the flowers (or just the stamens) very gently, and a small shower of pollen probably will come out.

Strong winds can carry pollen long distances.

There are records of pollen traveling several hundred miles, or even a few thousand miles, this way. In forests, however, pollen grains probably do not travel more than a few hundred feet.

The wind blows very little pollen directly from flower to flower. Most pollen transported by wind—in fact, nearly all of it—never reaches plants of the same species. Most of it falls on the ground or is blown out to sea. Some lands on other plants or on animals. Even if the pollen reaches a plant of the right species, it may settle on some part other than a stigma. Only an extremely small fraction of the wind-blown pollen grains actually lands on a receptive stigma. The large losses do not matter much, because wind-pollinated plants produce great quantities of pollen. It has been estimated that a single corn plant produces 20 to 50 million pollen grains.

For this reason, wind-pollinated plants are often described as being wasteful of pollen. Yet many of them have adaptations that prevent pollen from being released on windless days when it would be wasted by dropping directly to the ground. In corn, for example, the anthers are curved in such a way that there is a little spoon-shaped ledge below each pore. On calm days, the pollen falls on these ledges. As more and more of it accumulates, it blocks the pores. Later, when a breeze tilts the anthers, the pollen falls from the ledges and the pores are no longer blocked.

The pistils of wind-pollinated plants often have large, fuzzy, or branched stigmas. This increases the surface area on which pollen grains can land and still be used. Notice especially the pistils of corn and wheatgrass (page 20). The ovaries usually have only one ovule. Wind distributes pollen far and wide, and a given pistil is likely to receive only a few pollen grains. If the pistil had many ovules, there would not be enough pollen tubes growing down the style to reach all of them.

Some other wind-pollinated plants are elm, ash, alder, hickory, hazelnut, beech, birch, many grasses, ragweed, hops, and cattail. Pine, spruce, hemlock, and other cone-bearing trees do not have flowers but do have male cones that produce pollen and female cones that have ovules; pollination of these is by wind, too.

One thing you may have noticed about wind-pollinated flowers is that many of them are not particularly attractive to our eyes. You would not choose to pick them for a bouquet or a corsage. In fact, the pollen of these plants is responsible for many types of hay fever. If any of the plants mentioned in this chapter are planted by human beings, it is for their shade, their fruits and seeds, or some other feature we find desirable, but it is rarely for the appearance of their flowers.

There is nothing a farmer or gardener can do to encourage the wind to blow more in order to get better pollination. He can, however, plant all the plants of a wind-pollinated species close together in order to get better pollination. If you have a backyard garden and want to raise only one or two dozen corn plants, it is best to plant them all in one small, square plot. Then pollen from any one of the corn plants is more likely to reach another corn plant. If you plant your seeds in one long row, the wind probably will blow the pollen away from the row, and few ears will produce kernels.

· Pollination · by Animals

Animals do not visit flowers to pollinate them, for animals do not know that flowers need to be pollinated if they are to produce seeds and fruits. Animals visit flowers for other reasons, most commonly to secure food, but sometimes to find mates or to lay eggs.

Bees and other insects that feed their young require protein-rich food like pollen; and as they collect pollen, some of it accumulates on their bodies and accidentally brushes off onto other things they touch, including stigmas. In this way, both the plant and the insect benefit. The loss of some pollen to the insect does little harm to the plant, and the loss is more than offset by the advantage of pollination. The insects, in turn, have benefited by obtaining food.

Many animal-pollinated flowers produce *nectar*, a

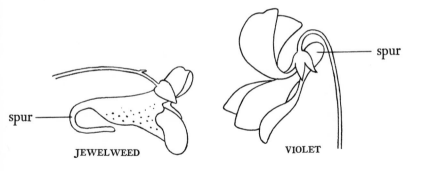

spur

spur

JEWELWEED   VIOLET

sweet mixture consisting of sugar and water, and this may be a greater attraction than pollen to many animals. Not only insects, but also a few birds and bats, visit flowers to obtain nectar. Usually the nectar is produced and stored in the base of the flower, and to reach it, the animal must brush past both the anthers and the stigmas. In columbine, violets, pansies, jewelweed, and butter-and-eggs, the nectar is stored in a spur.

Nectar is usually hidden from sight in the depth of a flower, and nectar-producing flowers often have color patterns, called *nectar guides*, that surround or point to the opening that the animal must enter before it can reach the nectar. In butter-and-eggs, the nectar guide is a spot of orange color. In violets and irises, it consists of lines pointing the way toward the nectar. The "face" on a pansy flower is a nectar guide. In Turk's-cap lilies, a cluster of spots in the center of the flower attracts the pollinating insect. A star-shaped pattern surrounds the opening to the nectar in morning glories, bindweeds, and petunias.

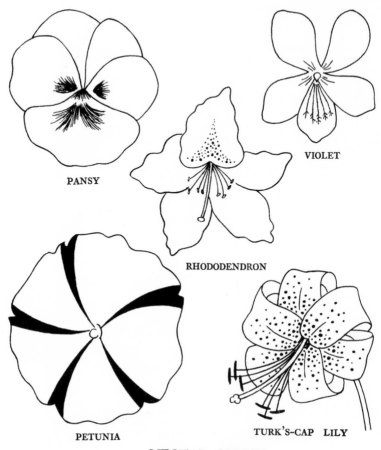

PANSY

VIOLET

RHODODENDRON

PETUNIA

TURK'S-CAP LILY

NECTAR GUIDES

Even if they don't have nectar guides, many animal-pollinated flowers have large, brightly colored, showy petals; scarlet sage, cannas, and some lilies are examples. If the flowers are small, they may be crowded into showy inflorescences as they are in milkweeds, Queen Anne's lace, sunflowers, and clovers.

The size and color of the flowers helps the animal to "learn" a certain flower. Bees, for instance, usually visit just one species of plant at a time. If both pear trees and maple trees are in bloom side by side, a bee will spend a great deal of time going from pear flower to pear flower or from maple flower to maple flower, but it will not go back and forth between pear and maple flowers. This helps to prevent wasting of pollen, for then pear pollen is not carried to maple trees, nor maple pollen to pear trees.

Many animal-pollinated flowers produce odors when they secrete nectar or when their pollen is ripe. The animals soon learn to associate these odors with food and come to collect it. At night, when there is not enough light to see colors, odor is a better attractant than color.

Pollen carried by animals usually is large and sticky or spiny. The pollen grains clump together and stick to the body of the visiting animal. The animals usually are covered by hair, fur, or feathers on which pollen can become caught. It is not likely to fall off as the animal travels between flowers.

There is much less pollen produced in animal-pollinated flowers than in wind-pollinated ones. Because the pollinating animals move more or less directly from flower to flower, the pollen is not distributed far and wide as it is in wind pollination. Not so much pollen is wasted and, therefore, not so much is needed.

The stigmas of animal-pollinated flowers are more

compact than they are in wind-pollinated flowers, but the flowers are so constructed that the pollinating animal can hardly avoid brushing against a receptive stigma. The pistils usually have at least several ovules, and often hundreds or even thousands. Because an animal carries many pollen grains at one time, if pollination does occur, the stigma is likely to receive many pollen grains and not just one. With many ovules in a pistil, most of these pollen grains will be used and not wasted. One pollination by just one animal then can result in the production of many seeds.

Not all animals that visit flowers pollinate them. Bees, for instance, collect pollen from corn tassels, but because nothing in the ears interests them, they do not visit the pistillate flowers. This does not mean that an animal could not pollinate plants that ordinarily are wind-pollinated, but it happens only rarely.

Ants love sugar, and you may often see them moving in and out of flowers to take nectar. Because they are so small, they usually reach the nectar without touching either the anthers or the stigmas. Even if they do, most ants could not carry pollen very far, for they have hard, smooth outer surfaces, and most pollen grains could not stick to them.

Animals that take nectar from flowers without pollinating them are called robbers. Even animals that ordinarily pollinate certain flowers may, on occasion, bypass the stigmas and anthers and steal nectar. Bees sometimes learn to bite into the base of a corolla tube and sip nectar through the hole. Later, if there is nectar left or if the flower continues to produce more, other robbers may take advantage of the hole, too. If a flower has separate petals, a bee or butterfly may merely rest next to the flower, insert its proboscis between the petals, and sip the nectar.

A little bit of robbery may not harm the plants; in fact, as we shall see on page 123, it may even be beneficial. However, if a great deal of nectar is lost, then there may not be enough left to attract the real pollinators, and this will reduce greatly the number of seeds produced by the plants.

Some flowers are protected against robbers by a dense covering of hairs on the stem, which blocks the way upward for small, crawling insects. If the hairs are sticky, they may also trap flying insects as well. One such plant is called catchfly. Other plants are protected in other ways. Some cherries and vetches produce an extra supply of nectar on their leaves; this decoys ants and other sugar-loving insects away from the flowers. On some tropical plants, ants lured by nectar to the stems or leaves attack other robbers and so protect the flowers.

The flowers of teasel are protected from crawling insects by the leaves, which occur in pairs. The two leaves of each pair are on opposite sides of the stem, and they are fused together, forming a bowl. When this bowl fills with dew or rainwater, small insects crawling up the stem find their way blocked by a little moat.

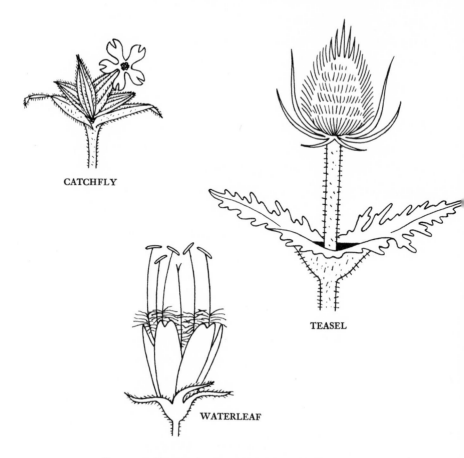

CATCHFLY

TEASEL

WATERLEAF

In snapdragons, the closed mouth of the corolla can be forced open by large, strong insects like bees, which then pollinate the flowers; but small robbers cannot get in. If you examine flowers with tubular or funnel-shaped corollas, you will find that some of them contain hairs; in some cases the hairs guide pollinators into the flower, but in other cases they block the way to robbers.

If a farmer or gardener knows what animals pollinate his plants, he can often get better pollination by encouraging the animals to live near his fields or garden. Allowing small nearby woodlots or narrow strips of land at the edges of a field to grow wild can provide nesting places for small animals. If a large farm is planted to just one crop plant, which blooms at only one time of year, the presence of some wild, uncultivated land may be of special advantage, for the bees or other pollinators must find food when the crop is not in bloom. Wild flowers (including weeds) that bloom at other times of the year can provide this food. Flowers that bloom at the same time as the crop plants, however, may be more attractive to the animals than are the crop plants; in this case, farmers find they get better pollination if they mow down the wild flowers at that time. Because bees, especially honeybees, pollinate so many of our common food crops, farmers often provide wooden shelters in which bees can build their hives.

The use of insecticides to kill harmful insects nearly always reduces the amount of pollination, for the pollinating insects are killed, too. This should be avoided whenever possible. Farmers sometimes must rent beehives during pollination time if the wild bees have been killed.

The next chapters discuss some examples of pollination by bees, wasps, other insects, and other animals. You should remember that while some flowers can be pollinated by only one species of animal, others may be pollinated by several.

· Pollination ·
by Bees

Many animals are color-blind, but bees see most of the colors we do. They see yellow, blue, blue-green, and violet very well, and many bee flowers are yellow or blue. Bees do not see red, which looks like black to them, and so it is not surprising that very few bee flowers are red. But bees do see one "color" that is invisible to us: ultraviolet. So if a flower reflects ultraviolet light, bees can see it. For a long time biologists were puzzled by the fact that bees visit the bright red poppies so common in Europe. Then it was discovered that the poppies reflect ultraviolet light as well as red light, and it was this and not the red light that attracted the bees. We, on the other hand, see the red light from these flowers, but not the ultraviolet.

Flowers that appear to us to be uniformly colored

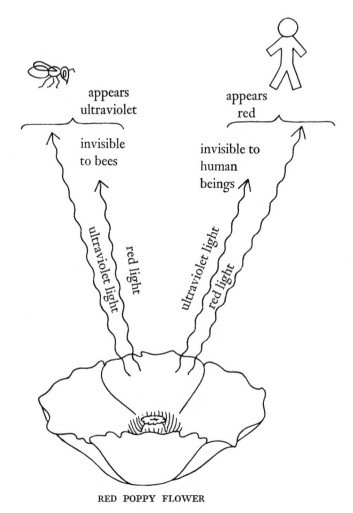

appears
ultraviolet

appears
red

invisible
to bees

invisible to
human
beings

ultraviolet light

red light

ultraviolet light

red light

RED POPPY FLOWER

may possess nectar guides visible to bees. We see marsh marigold flowers simply as yellow flowers because they reflect yellow light, which is visible to us. However, the outer parts of marsh marigold flowers also reflect ultraviolet light, though the central part

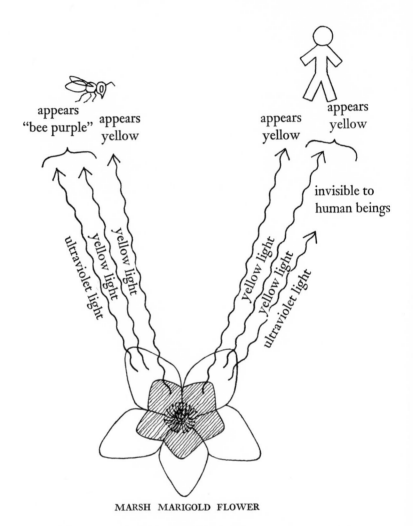

MARSH MARIGOLD FLOWER

of the flowers does not. The bee sees one of these flowers as having a yellow center and an outer part of mixed yellow and ultraviolet light, called "bee purple." We have no better name for this mixture, because we ourselves do not see the mixture (only the yellow part of it), and so we do not know exactly how it looks to a bee.

The odors of many bee flowers attract bees and generally are quite pleasant to us as well. Orange blossoms have such a delightful odor that brides carry them in their bouquets. Cherry and plum blossoms are more delicately scented. The odors of clovers, especially the sweet clovers, drift pleasantly over farm fields and country roadsides on a warm summer day.

Most bee flowers (or the inflorescences, in the case of some small flowers) are large enough and strong enough to support a bee as it walks over or crawls into them. Usually, but not always, there is a landing place on which the bee alights first. The landing place may be the whole flower, only part of the flower, or an entire inflorescence.

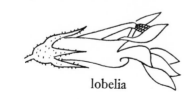

lobelia

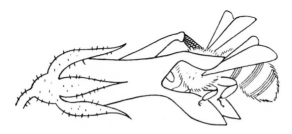

bee lands on lower lip
of lobelia flower

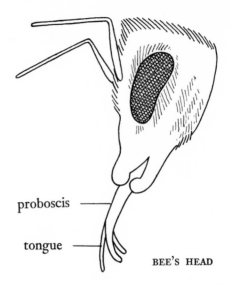

proboscis

tongue

BEE'S HEAD

Bees collect nectar by sucking it up with a long, tubular mouth part called a *proboscis*. Inside the proboscis is a slender tongue that the bee can extend into narrow flowers. The longer the tongue, the deeper the bee can probe for nectar.

Depending on the location of the anthers in the flower, a bee may receive pollen on any part of its body: head, back, or underside. If you watch bees working in flowers, you should observe them when they leave a flower in order to see where they actually receive pollen. From time to time the bee cleans its body and moves the pollen grains to a special set of hairs, called a *pollen basket,* on its hind legs. When the pollen basket is full, the bee returns to the hive and leaves the pollen there before going out to visit more flowers.

Because there are so many bee-pollinated flowers only a few examples can be examined here, but do remember that bees are the most important pollinators of our food crops as well as of many wild plants. The following are pollinated only by bees or primarily by bees: apple, pear, cherry, plum, peach, watermelon, cantaloupe, squash, pumpkin, cucumber, strawberry, raspberry, blackberry, blueberry, cranberry, avocado, carrot, cabbage, broccoli, Brussels sprouts, onion, passion fruit, and buckwheat. Clovers and alfalfa, which are used as animal feed, are pollinated by bees,

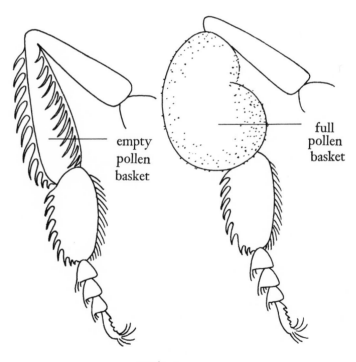

empty pollen basket

full pollen basket

BEE'S HIND LEG

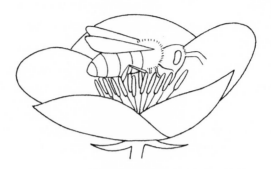

BEE ON BUTTERCUP FLOWER

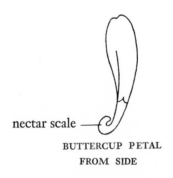

nectar scale

BUTTERCUP PETAL
FROM SIDE

as are cotton plants. Although green beans, lima beans, peanuts, and soybeans usually are self-pollinated, bees occasionally cross-pollinate them, too.

One of the simplest pollination stories is that of the buttercup. The many pistils in the center of a buttercup flower are surrounded by a ring of many stamens. Each of the five yellow petals of the flower has near its base a small scale under which nectar is stored. Bees searching in the flower for nectar can hardly help brushing against several stigmas and anthers during a visit. Although this causes some self-pollination, it brings about cross-pollination, too, as the bees travel from plant to plant.

Flowers with pistils and stamens freely exposed like this may also be pollinated by flies and other insects, although bees usually are the most important pollinators.

The snapdragon is such a popular garden plant that it should not be difficult for you to find one in bloom some warm summer day when bees are about. A bee usually lands on the lower lip of the corolla, and then forces its way into the mouth of the flower. If you watch a bee entering and leaving several snapdragon flowers, you should see that it carries a good deal of pollen on its back. Stick your finger into a snapdragon flower—be sure first there's no bee in the flower. The side of your finger corresponding to the bee's back will have the most pollen on it when you remove it from the flower.

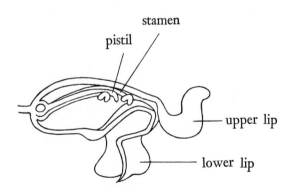

LONGITUDINAL SECTION
OF SNAPDRAGON FLOWER

With a sharp razor blade, cut a flower into two halves as shown in the illustration. Notice that the stigma and the anthers are all in the upper half of the flower. In what direction does the stigma face? As a bee forces the mouth open and squeezes into the flower, the bee's back touches the stigma and the anthers. If the bee carries pollen from a flower it visited previously, some of it may brush off onto the stigma. At the same time, the bee also receives fresh pollen.

Japanese barberry is a thorny shrub often used as a hedge. It blooms in late spring or early summer. Its small yellowish flowers have six sepals, six petals, six stamens, and one pistil. You should be able to find two orange nectar glands near the base of each petal. The stamens curve outward a little, and if the flower has not been visited recently by a bee, each stamen nestles against one of the petals.

As a visiting bee approaches a nectar gland, its proboscis will touch the stigma and deposit some of the pollen it carries. The proboscis is also very likely to touch one of the filaments. When this happens, the filament snaps upward and toward the center of the flower, and the anther hits the bee's proboscis. You can see how this works if you substitute a pencil for the bee. Just touch a filament gently with a sharp pencil point. Then examine the pencil point for pollen grains.

If a bee touches the stigma with the front of its proboscis, it receives pollen on the back of the

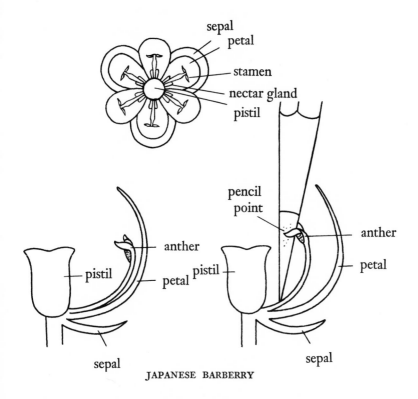

JAPANESE BARBERRY

proboscis. If the bee extends its proboscis over the pistil to reach the nectar glands on the far side of the flower, then it will touch the stigma with the back of the proboscis and receive pollen on the front. After visiting a few Japanese barberry flowers, the bee has pollen dusted on all sides of its proboscis; then, no matter where in a flower it searches for nectar, it probably will leave some pollen on the stigma.

Blue meadow sage has a pollination story that requires two visits by bees for its completion. The corolla forms a tube something like that of a snapdragon. There are an upper lip and a lower lip around the mouth, but the mouth is wide open. The pistil and the two stamens lie under the upper lip. Each stamen has a short filament and an unusual anther. Instead of consisting of two similar halves as most other anthers do, a blue meadow sage anther has two unequal halves. One half is short, flat, and sterile; the other half is elongated into a stalk (which can easily be mistaken for a filament) that ends in an anther sac. This entire anther can tilt back and forth on its filament, but, unless disturbed, it stands under

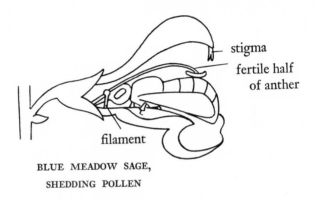

stigma

fertile half
of anther

filament

BLUE MEADOW SAGE,
SHEDDING POLLEN

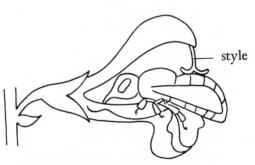

style

BLUE MEADOW SAGE,
STIGMAS RECEPTIVE

the upper lip as shown in the illustration. The style has two stigmas. When the pollen is ripe, the two stigmas press against each other and are not receptive.

A bee visiting a blue meadow sage flower lands on the lower lip and then enters the flower to take nectar. The lower, sterile parts of the anthers lie in the bee's way, and as the bee's head pushes against them, the anthers tilt on their filaments and the open anther sacs land on the bee's back and cover it with pollen.

A day or two later, the style has grown a little longer, and the two stigmas become receptive and spread apart. They bend down to almost exactly the same position previously occupied by the anthers as they hit the bee. When a bee now visits the flowers, the stigmas receive some pollen from the bee's back. This pollen, of course, came from a different flower, a flower that is in the same stage (shedding pollen) as the first flower was a day or two earlier. The pollen from one flower is deposited in just the right place on the bee's body for it to be transferred most efficiently to the stigma of another flower.

Catalpa trees have flowers with stamens and pistils that mature at the same time but still prevent self-pollination. The corolla forms a tube with a wide-open mouth. There are two stamens and one pistil, which is longer than the stamens. The pistil has two stigmas, spread so far apart that they curve backward toward the style. A bee lands on the lower lip of the corolla, then enters the flower. The bee touches the stigmas first and brushes onto them any pollen

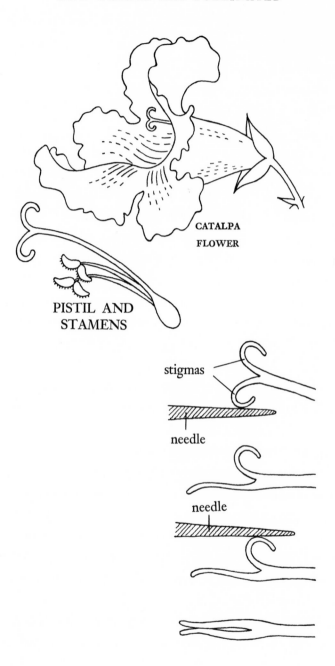

CATALPA
FLOWER

PISTIL AND
STAMENS

stigmas

needle

needle

it may be carrying. Immediately after being touched, the two stigmas come together, hiding their receptive surfaces between them. Then, as the bee touches the anthers, picks up fresh pollen, and passes the stigmas on its way out of the flower, it cannot pollinate the flower with its own pollen.

Catalpa trees (also called Indian bean or cigar trees because of their long seed pods) are planted along some city streets. They bloom early in summer. If you can find one with flowers low enough for you to reach, you can observe the closing mechanism of the stigmas. All you have to do is to touch an open stigma with a pencil point or a needle and watch the stigmas close against each other. They will open again within a few minutes—but the time elapsed has been long enough for a bee to complete its visit and depart.

Shooting stars are wild flowers of late spring or early summer. They are most common in prairies and in mountainous country. The flowers hang upside down, and the anthers are fused to each other and form a cone pointing downward. Mature anthers have open slits on their inner sides. Pollen shed by the anthers accumulates inside the cone until a bee disturbs the flower. The style extends through the cone and beyond it. Thus the stigma is the lowest part of the upside-down flower. When a bee (usually a bumblebee) lands on a shooting star flower, it, too, hangs upside down, for this is one of the few bee flowers that lacks a good landing place, and the bee must cling to the anther cone. The lower surface of

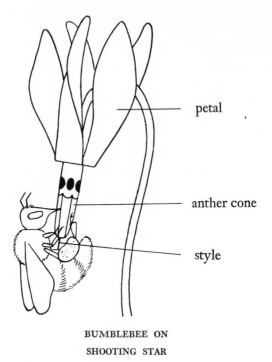

petal

anther cone

style

BUMBLEBEE ON
SHOOTING STAR

the bee touches the stigma and deposits on it some of
the pollen it may be carrying. As the bee beats its
wings while hanging from the flower, it shakes the
flower and this causes pollen grains to fall from the
open anthers onto the lower surface of its body.

Another plant with similar flowers pollinated in
the same way is bittersweet nightshade, a common
weed. The only difference is that its anthers open by
pores at their tips rather than by slits, as the shooting
star anthers do. The pollen falls out when a bee shakes
the flower.

The flowers of tomato plants look like those of
shooting stars and bittersweet nightshade, but most

tomato flowers are self-pollinated. The pistil is shorter than the anthers and does not extend out of the anther cone. The anthers develop slits that open to the inside of the cone, and because the anthers fit so closely together, pollen does not escape from the flower. When wind or a visiting insect shakes the flower, some of the pollen falls on the stigma. Tomato plants grown in greenhouses must be artificially shaken, otherwise they usually are not pollinated and so do not produce fruit.

Beans, peas, lupines, clovers, and their relatives form a large family of flowering plants called the bean family. Their flowers differ somewhat in size and color, but each has one large petal called a *standard*, two petals called *wings*, and two petals

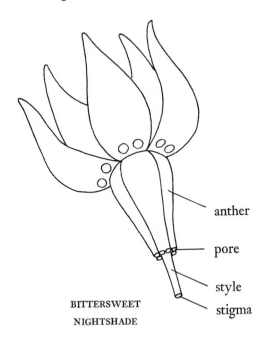

anther

pore

style

stigma

BITTERSWEET
NIGHTSHADE

united into a *keel*, the shape of which resembles the keels of some boats. The keel encloses ten stamens and one pistil.

Although bees pollinate flowers of most members of this family, there are several somewhat different pollination stories.

Everlasting pea (sometimes called sweet pea, though it is not a true sweet pea and does not have the delightful scent of sweet peas) is a common garden flower. The petals may be red, white, or rose-colored. When a bee approaches a flower, it lands on the keel, which bends downward under the bee's weight. This exposes the stamens and pistils.

You can see how the flower works if you pick one; with one hand, hold the flower by its base, and with the other, press down on the keel at about its middle with a finger or pencil. The stamens and pistil will emerge at the end of the keel. You should be able to see something unusual for a cross-pollinated flower; the anthers will have already opened and shed their pollen on the pistil. But if you look more closely, you will see exactly where on the pistil most of the pollen is. The upper part of the style bears a tuft of hairs called the *stylar brush*, and this will be yellow with pollen. The stigma, which is at the tip of the style, is difficult to distinguish from the stylar brush unless you have a hand lens.

When a bee depresses the keel, it receives pollen, not so much directly from the anthers themselves, but mostly from the stylar brush. At the same time, the

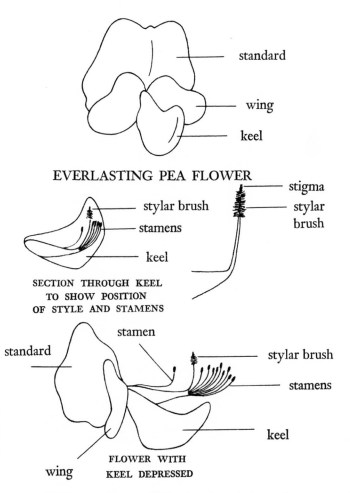

EVERLASTING PEA FLOWER

standard
wing
keel

stylar brush
stamens
keel

stigma
stylar brush

SECTION THROUGH KEEL
TO SHOW POSITION
OF STYLE AND STAMENS

stamen
standard
stylar brush
stamens
keel
wing
FLOWER WITH
KEEL DEPRESSED

stigma receives pollen the bee brings from another flower.

The pollination story of lupine is similar to that of everlasting pea, but differs in a few details. The two petals of the keel are fused at both the upper and lower edges; only a small opening is left at the tip of the keel. As the anthers shed their pollen, it accumulates inside the keel. When a bee depresses the keel, pollen oozes out onto the bee's body much as tooth-paste oozes onto your toothbrush when you squeeze the toothpaste tube.

The clovers have simpler pollination stories; the pollen is transferred directly from the anthers to the bee's body. Red clover and white clover are common weeds throughout the United States; each has a spherical inflorescence bearing several flowers, each barely large enough for you to work it. Red clover

standard
wing
keel

RED CLOVER FLOWER

stigma
stamen

LONGITUDINAL SECTION OF KEEL

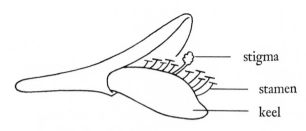

stigma
stamen
keel

FLOWER WITH KEEL
DEPRESSED, WING REMOVED

is the larger of the two; and its flowers are rosy-red. White clover is very common in lawns; its flowers are white or pale pink. If you remove one flower from either of these plants, depress the keel with a fingernail, and you will see that the stamens and stigma are all exposed and would brush against the underside of a bee working among the flowers.

A number of members of the bean family are regularly self-pollinated: green beans, lima beans, soybeans, peas, sweet peas, and peanuts. Many of those that are cross-pollinated by insects may be self-pollinated, too (but not the red and white clovers). It certainly is not hard to see how self-pollination might come about, especially in those species like everlasting pea and lupine, which release pollen directly into the keel where it touches the pistil before a bee ever visits the flower.

Lady's slippers are relatively rare orchids found in rich moist woods and bogs throughout most of the United States. They should not be picked, but the flowers are big, and you can see a lot without picking them. They bloom in late spring and in early summer. Each flower has three sepals (two are fused together and appear as one) and three petals. As with all orchids, one of the petals is distinctly different from the others; it is called the *labellum*. In lady's slipper's it forms a pouch that resembles a slipper in its shape.

In the center of the flower is a *column* composed of two fertile stamens, one sterile stamen, and the style and stigma. This column partially blocks the

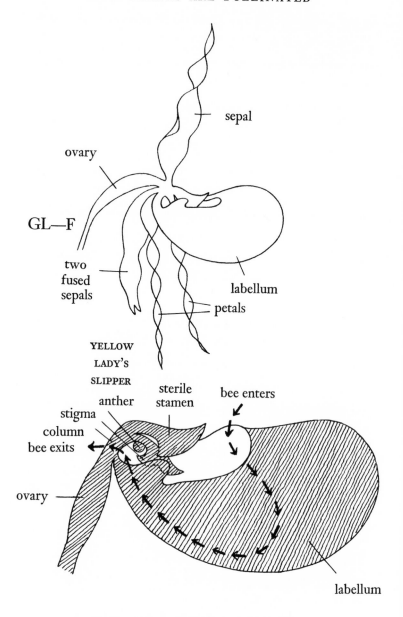

YELLOW LADY'S SLIPPER FLOWER WITH
SEPALS AND TWO PETALS REMOVED

opening of the pouch, and as a result there are three pathways into the pouch: two small spaces on either side of the column, and a larger one in front of it. A bee enters by way of the larger space. Once inside the pouch the bee cannot fly, for there is not enough room to do so. Instead, it must crawl out. But it cannot leave by the way it came in, for the areas of the pouch leading to the large opening are too slippery. The bee can, however, squeeze through one of the smaller spaces on either side of the column. As it does so, it cannot avoid touching the stigma and then one of the stamens. The pollen grains of lady's slippers are so sticky that all the pollen grains in one anther sac stay together in a sticky mass. A bee leaving a lady's slipper flower usually carries the entire mass of pollen grains smeared on its body. When it visits the next lady's slipper flower, much of this pollen mass is smeared on the stigma as the bee leaves that flower.

Bees visit the *Gongora* orchid of the tropics not for food but for what, from our human point of view, we might describe as becoming intoxicated. Compared with the lady's slipper flower, the *Gongora* flower appears to be upside down. The labellum is above the column, which curves downward in a shape like that of a playground slide, and it is just about as slippery. There is only one fertile anther; it and the stigma are near the tip of the column. The pollen grains of this orchid, as is true of most orchids, are enclosed in two little sacs called *pollinia*. Each pollinium has a short stalk with a sticky tip.

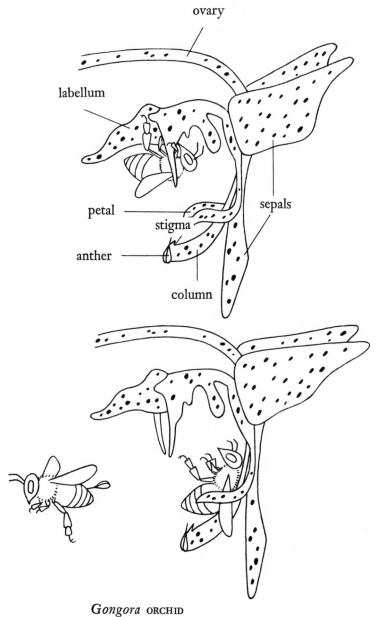

Gongora ORCHID

The intoxicating material that the bee seeks is in the labellum, and to get it, the bee must hang upside down and scratch the labellum with its forelegs. Because of "prongs" on either side of the labellum, the bee hangs directly over the column. As the bee becomes intoxicated from the substances released by the labellum, it loses its grip, falls on its back onto the column, and slides down the column past the stigma and anther. As it passes the anther, the sticky ends of the pollinia become attached to the back of the bee. After the bee recovers and is "sober," it flies to another *Gongora* flower where the same process is repeated. As the bee slides down the column, the pollinia already on its back become smashed against the stigma; this releases many pollen grains onto the stigma at one time. A fraction of a second later, as the bee passes the anther, it picks up new pollinia.

The flowers of another tropical orchid, *Oncidium*, resemble male bees enough that real bees mistake them for other bees. Becoming angry with what must appear to them to be invaders of their territories, the male bees attack the flowers by flying directly at them, battering them with their heads. This might be enough to drive away real bees, but the flowers, of course, remain where they are. As an angry bee attacks flower after flower, it picks up pollinia on its head and smashes them on to the stigmas of other flowers.

Milkweeds have one of the most interesting and

unusual methods of pollination. The flowers are small, but usually grouped into large inflorescences. Many are pink or lavender, a few are pale green. One species, called butterfly weed, is bright orange or yellow; it is pollinated by butterflies in much the same way that bees pollinate other milkweeds.

The five sepals and five petals of a milkweed flower bend downward, away from the other flower parts. Then, where you would ordinarily expect to find the stamens of a flower, milkweeds have an extra structure called a *corona*. It consists of five hoods, each with a horn in its center. The hoods hold nectar. In the center of the flower are the pistil and five stamens, which are fused with the pistil. The five stigmas of the pistil are inside slits spaced around the pistil rather than at the top of it. These stigma slits alternate in position with the anthers. The pollen grains in each anther are enclosed in two pollinia resembling the pollinia of orchids. One additional peculiarity of the milkweed flower is that a small black gland above each stigma slit joins two pollinia from two *different* anthers on either side of a stigma.

When a bee in search of nectar in the hoods approaches a milkweed flower, the bee usually rests one of its legs on the top of the pistil, but this is smooth and slippery, and the bee's leg slips off. Sometimes it slides into one of the stigma slits. As the bee frees its leg by pulling upward, the leg catches the gland and pulls it away along with the two pollinia attached to it. Once they have been pulled out of

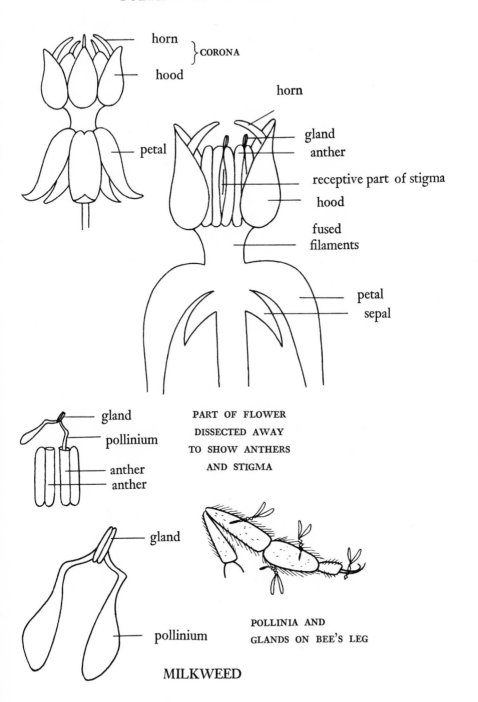

horn
}CORONA

hood

petal

horn

gland
anther

receptive part of stigma

hood

fused
filaments

petal
sepal

gland

pollinium

anther
anther

PART OF FLOWER
DISSECTED AWAY
TO SHOW ANTHERS
AND STIGMA

gland

pollinium

POLLINIA AND
GLANDS ON BEE'S LEG

MILKWEED

their anther sacs, the two pollinia begin to dry. As they do so, they twist around the bee's leg, thus securing themselves to the leg. They are not likely to fall when the bee flies from flower to flower. If the bee lands on another milkweed flower, and if its leg slips into a stigma slit again, the struggles of the bee to release itself breaks the pollinia and releases the pollen grains directly onto the stigma.

With a pin to imitate the bee's leg, you can remove the pollinia from milkweed flowers. An old pin with a rough surface would be a little more like a bee's bristly leg than would a new, smooth one. Look for the gland, which appears as a tiny black dot above a stigma slit. (If the gland is missing, a bee was there before you and removed it and the pollinia. Find another one.) Insert the tip of the pin in the stigma slit, and raise it up under the gland. As you pull the gland up, the pollinia will slide out of their anther sacs. If the weather is dry, hold the pin in the air for a while and watch the pollinia twist around the pin.

· Pollination ·
by Wasps

Wasps look a little like bees, but there are differences between them. For one thing, wasp bodies are not hairy like those of bees, and so wasps do not ordinarily carry pollen dusted over them as bees do. They also tend to visit flowers with dull, drab colors. Wasps visit flowers for several reasons: to obtain food, to find a mate, and to lay eggs.

Several helleborine orchids, European wild flowers, are visited by wasps. The labellum of this orchid has a small bowl-shaped depression that holds nectar. As a wasp clings to the labellum and sips the nectar, its head moves up and down, occasionally bumping into the stigma and anther. The sticky ends of the pollinia become attached to the wasp's head. For a while they stand straight out from the head, but after a while they begin to droop a little. Because the stigma is just a little lower on the column than the anther, when the wasp visits a second flower, the pollinia are in just the right position to be pressed against the stigma as the wasp drinks nectar from the labellum.

One of these helleborine orchids was accidentally introduced into the United States several years ago.

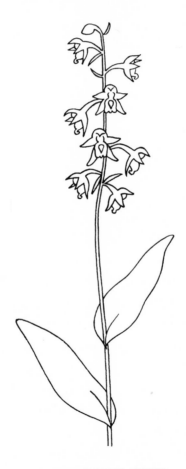

HELLEBORINE ORCHID

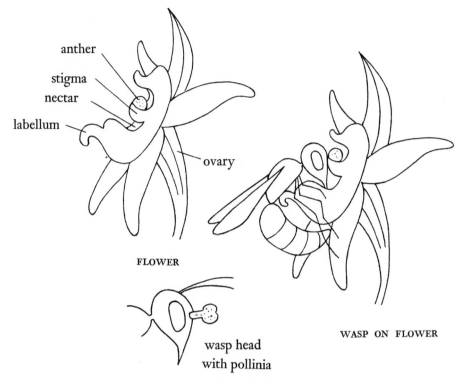

anther

stigma

nectar

labellum

ovary

FLOWER

wasp head
with pollinia

WASP ON FLOWER

No one knows exactly when or how, but it has spread throughout much of the northeastern United States in recent years. It usually grows at the edges of woods, where it receives sun from one side and shade from the other. Many persons consider the plants a weed, for the small flowers are a dull greenish brown. When you look closely at them, however, you can see that they are beautiful orchid flowers.

Another European wild orchid, *Ophrys speculum*, attracts wasps in a different way. The labellum of this flower produces no nectar. Rather, it resembles a

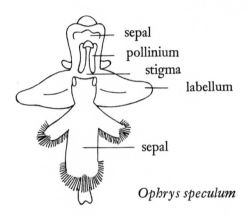

Ophrys speculum

female wasp. It takes only a little imagination to see the head, wings, and abdomen of the imitation female wasp. The flower even produces an odor similar to that of the female wasp. A male wasp seeking a mate may be deceived by a flower. In his attempt to mate with the flower, the male wasp bumps his head against the stigma and anther, and the pollinia stick to its head. Having discovered his mistake, he flies off, still seeking a female wasp. Quite likely he will be deceived by other *Ophrys speculum* flowers and attempt to mate with them, each time depositing pollinia and receiving new ones.

Of course, not all male wasps are unsuccessful in finding a mate. Otherwise there would be no more of these wasps, and neither would there be any of the orchids they pollinate.

There are other species of *Ophrys* that resemble female bees, and these are pollinated by male bees.

One of the most complex pollination stories is that of the cultivated fig, which is native to the lands around the Mediterranean Sea. There are two varieties of this tree. One variety, called the Smyrna fig, produces edible figs. The other, called the caprifig, produces inedible figs. Around 1880 Smyrna fig trees were brought to California (where they are now called Calimyrna figs), but for many years the trees bore no figs. It was only after the pollination story of these figs became known, that it was understood that caprifig trees and fig wasps were necessary for pollination of the Smyrna figs. When these two necessary components were imported to California in 1899, the Smyrna fig trees began producing figs.

The fig tree bears inflorescences, each consisting of many minute flowers almost completely surrounded by a stem that grows around them. Only at the top of the inflorescence is there a small hole through which the tiny fig wasps can enter or leave. The Smyrna fig has only pistillate flowers. Each flower consists of one pistil surrounded by several perianth parts. The pistillate flowers are so close together that there is no space left between them. The pistils in these fig flowers have long styles that extend far beyond the perianth parts. If you cut through a dried Smyrna fig, which is a ripe inflorescence, you can see many tiny individual fruits (which look like seeds). Each of these is still surrounded by the old perianth parts.

The caprifig flowers differ slightly from those of the Smyrna figs. A caprifig inflorescence contains both staminate and pistillate flowers. The staminate flowers are all near the opening of the inflorescence, and the pistillate flowers have styles shorter than those in the Smyrna figs.

When a female fig wasp enters a caprifig, she lays her eggs in the ovaries of the pistillate flowers. This destroys the ovules, and so these flowers produce no seeds, but the wasp larvae find all the food they need there inside the inflorescence. When the young wasps become adults, the males are wingless, but the females have wings. The males never leave the caprifigs but find the females and mate with them there. The

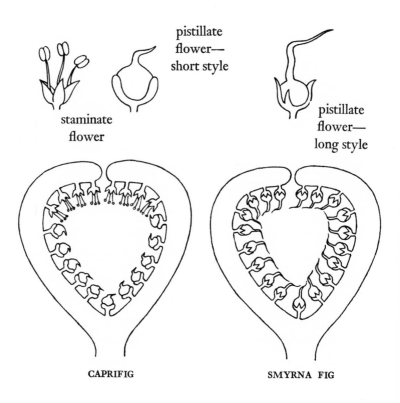

pistillate flower— short style

staminate flower

pistillate flower— long style

CAPRIFIG

SMYRNA FIG

females then crawl out of the narrow opening in the caprifig. In doing so, they collect pollen grains from the staminate flowers, which do not shed their pollen until this time. The female wasps fly to other figs in search of a place to lay their eggs. If one enters a caprifig, the process just described is repeated, but if she enters a Smyrna fig, a different part of the pollination story is begun.

The long styles of the Smyrna fig flowers prevent the wasp from laying her eggs in the ovaries of these pistils, and so no wasp larvae develop there. The pollen the wasp carries from the caprifigs does pollinate these long-styled flowers, and so the Smyrna figs produce seed.

Ordinarily this entire pollination story is repeated three times a year, and three crops of figs, both caprifigs and Smyrna figs, are produced—one crop of each in spring, in summer, and in autumn.

For a long time, no one knew how female fig wasps carried pollen, for their outer surfaces are too smooth to hold pollen grains, and the wasps usually clean themselves as soon as they force their way out of the caprifigs. Then one day, a biologist studying these wasps accidentally squashed one, and several thousand pollen grains came out of the body. After a little investigation, he discovered two pouches in the wasp's body in which she carried the pollen.

Although caprifigs are not edible, they are necessary for two reasons: they provide the pollen necessary for pollinating Smyrna fig flowers; and they provide a home for the developing wasps that carry pollen to the Smyrna fig flowers. The fig trees and the fig wasps are completely dependent on each other. The fig flowers can be pollinated only by the fig wasp, and the fig wasp larvae can develop only in the caprifigs.

· Pollination by · Butterflies and Moths

Butterflies and moths look very much alike, and they do have some of the same habits. Both types of insect drink nectar through a slender proboscis that enables them to probe deeply into flowers with narrow, tubular corollas or long spurs. If stamens and pistils block the way to the nectar, butterflies and moths merely extend their proboscises beyond them and into the flower. Depending on the size of the insect and the length of the stamens, pollen is dusted on the proboscis or the main part of the body. When the insect is not feeding, it coils its proboscis out of the way under its mouth.

If you watch one of these insects feeding at the small flowers of an inflorescence, those of goldenrod for instance, you will notice a "knee bend" about the middle of the proboscis. The knee bend enables the

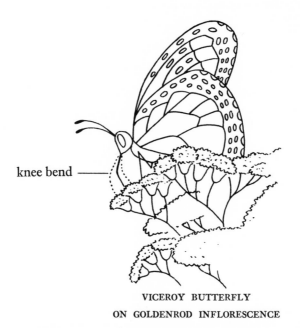

knee bend

VICEROY BUTTERFLY
ON GOLDENROD INFLORESCENCE

insect to move its proboscis from flower to flower in
the inflorescence without changing its own position.
This helps the insect to conserve energy.

Butterflies are active by day. They can see several
colors, but their sense of smell is not well developed.
Butterfly flowers are open by day and usually have
bright colors. Some examples are: larkspur, nastur-
tium, purple loosestrife, pinks, goldenrod, butterfly
weed, and some mints. If butterfly flowers are scented,
they usually have only light, delicate odors. Butterflies prefer to alight and rest while they feed, and
their flowers or inflorescences are large enough to
provide a resting-place.

Purple loosestrife flowers have an interesting arrangement of stamens and pistils that helps to prevent self-pollination and to increase the chance of cross-pollination. Each flower has one pistil, but some flowers have a short pistil, some a medium-length pistil, and some a long pistil. The difference in length is due primarily to the different lengths of the styles. Stamens, too, may be short, medium-length, or long—because of differences in the lengths of the filaments.

FRITILLARY BUTTERFLY
ON WILD BERGAMOT INFLORESCENCE

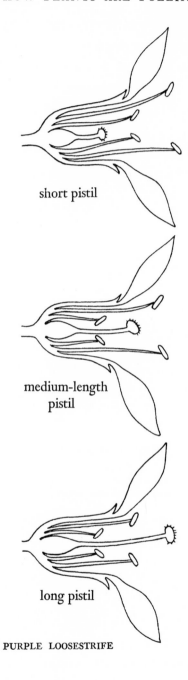

short pistil

medium-length
pistil

long pistil

PURPLE LOOSESTRIFE

Each flower has twelve stamens, six of one length and six of another.

Flowers with short pistils have six medium-length and six long stamens. Flowers with medium-length pistils have six short and six long stamens. Flowers with long pistils have six short and six medium-length stamens. In other words, no flower has stamens the same length as its pistil. Any purple loosestrife plant has flowers of only one type.

If you were to open one flower of each type and lay them side by side, you would see that the anthers of short stamens are at the same height in the flower as are the stigmas of short pistils. Similarly, anthers of medium-length stamens and stigmas of medium-length pistils are at the same height, and the same is true of long stamens and long pistils.

When a butterfly inserts its proboscis into a purple loosestrife flower, pollen is deposited on the proboscis at a position that corresponds to the height of the stigmas of other flowers, but not of the flowers of that plant. Thus if a butterfly visits a flower with a short pistil, the pollen it receives is in a good position for it to pollinate flowers with medium-length or long pistils, but not one with a short pistil. Similarly, when the butterfly visits a flower with a medium-length or long pistil the pollen it picks up is at a good place on the proboscis for pollination of other flowers, but not the same flower.

This is not the only thing that helps to prevent self-pollination in purple loosestrife. If you were to take pollen from a stamen of one length and place it on the stigma of a pistil of a different length, very few seeds would be produced, and very few of these would germinate. The best seeds result from pollination of pistils by pollen from stamens of the same length, and this pollen must come from stamens of flowers on other plants.

There are differences between butterflies and moths, and moth flowers are generally different from butterfly flowers. Most moths are active at twilight or during the night, when colors cannot be easily distinguished, and most moth flowers open at night and are pale in color. Evening primrose and some of the night-blooming cactuses are examples. Some moth flowers, such as honeysuckle, yucca, phlox, and rhododendrons, are open by day as well. Instead of attracting moths by color, moth flowers attract them primarily by emitting strong odors. Honeysuckle, gardenia, tuberoses, and some lilies and night-blooming cactuses produce scents that human beings find quite delightful, although some of the scents may be so strong that many persons tire of them quickly.

Many moths hover while they feed; that is, by beating their wings, they remain in one position in the air. Thus they do not need a place to rest, and most moth flowers do not have any landing platform. Moths take nectar quickly from a flower and pause only briefly before moving on to another flower. Turk's-cap lilies, which are pollinated by large hawkmoths, are good examples of flowers lacking landing

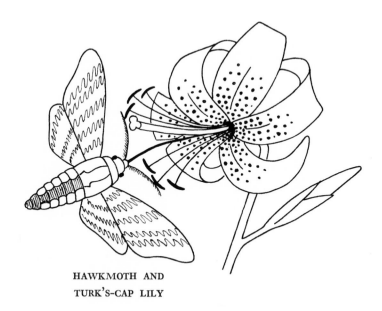

HAWKMOTH AND
TURK'S-CAP LILY

platforms. The pistil and the stamens are about the same length, and they extend well out from the rest of the flower. The hawkmoth's proboscis is about as long as the stamens and pistils. As the moth extends its proboscis to collect nectar from the bases of the tepals, its body brushes against the anthers and stigma.

Yucca plants (also called Spanish bayonet, Adam's needle, or Our Lord's candle) grow naturally only where a pale blue moth called the yucca moth lives, and the yucca moth lives only where yucca plants grow. This is because these two, like the fig and the fig wasp, are dependent on each other. Only female yucca moths pollinate yucca flowers, and yucca seeds are the only food of yucca moth larvae.

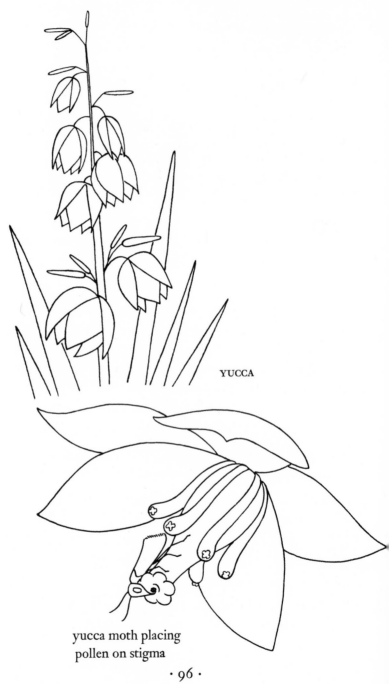

YUCCA

yucca moth placing
pollen on stigma

Unlike most other insects, the yucca moth does not pollinate by brushing accidentally against anthers and stigmas. Instead, she first gathers pollen from anthers and rolls it into a ball that she takes to another yucca flower. Here she lays a few eggs in the ovary of the pistil. Then she deposits the pollen on the stigma and pats it firmly into place. After pollination, the ovules develop into seeds. At the same time, the moth eggs develop into moth larvae. As the larvae grow, they feed on the seeds, but because there are so many seeds and so few larvae in each ovary, most of the seeds survive and next year may grow into new yucca plants. Some of the larvae become adult female yucca moths the next year and pollinate new yucca flowers.

· Pollination ·
by Other Insects

Flies are not among our favorite insects. One of their habits we find disgusting is walking on rotten meat or on dung (the excrement of animals) and laying their eggs there. Of course, for the fly, this is a valuable habit, for the larvae developing from the eggs find nourishment in the meat or the dung. We might suppose then that fly flowers look and smell like rotting meat or dung, and so they do.

The carrion-flower (the word *carrion* means rotting meat) is native to Africa, but occasionally is grown as a curiosity in greenhouses. You might find it also called *Stapelia* there. With its thick, green stems, it looks a little like a cactus. It has a large, star-shaped flower with five reddish-brown petals about the color of old, raw meat. Its carrionlike odor attracts flies, which are so deceived by it that they lay their eggs in the flowers. In so doing, they transfer pollen from flower to flower. Unlike the yucca moths, whose offspring grow in the seeds of the flower pollinated by the parent, flies derive no benefit from the pollination activity. The eggs may develop into larvae, but they soon die because they do not find proper food in the flowers.

The spotted arum lily of Europe traps flies and gnats for a few days and then releases them. During their imprisonment the flies pollinate the flowers. The tiny, spotted arum lily flowers grow on a special stem

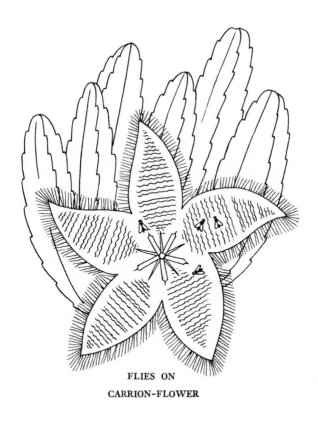

FLIES ON
CARRION-FLOWER

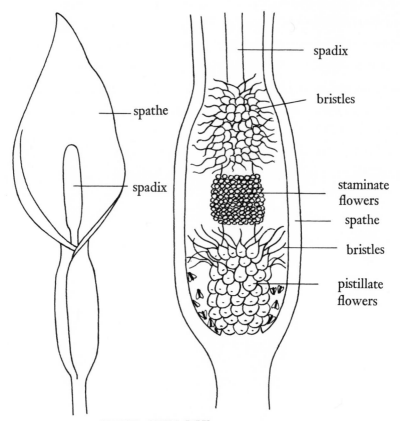

spadix

bristles

spathe

spadix

staminate
flowers

spathe

bristles

pistillate
flowers

SPOTTED ARUM LILY

called a *spadix*. The pistillate flowers are at the bottom of the spadix. Above them there is a ring of
bristles, and the staminate flowers are above these.
Then there is another ring of bristles, and the top
half of the spadix is bare. A modified leaf called a
spathe surrounds the spadix.

When the pistillate flowers are mature, the upper,
bare part of the spadix attracts flies and gnats by
emitting the odor of rotting meat. The spadix is very

slippery, and insects landing on it fall down into the spathe. There they are trapped, for the inside of the spathe is slippery, too, and so they cannot crawl out; neither can they fly away, for the bristles block the way out. In their trap, the insects feed on sticky substances secreted by the pistillate flowers. If they carry any pollen from another spotted arum lily, they pollinate the pistillate flowers. At the same time, they become covered with some of the sticky material.

The staminate flowers ripen next, and as they shed their pollen, it falls onto the now-sticky insects. Then the bristles begin to wilt, allowing the pollen-covered insects to escape from their trap. The spadix no longer produces its carrion odor and so the insects no longer stay there. If another spotted arum lily plant is emitting the odor now, the insects fly to it, and when they become trapped, they pollinate its pistillate flowers.

Beetle flowers have strong scents, too. The giant arum lily of Sumatra produces a gigantic inflorescence that reaches heights of 8 to 10 feet. This plant, which is pollinated by carrion beetles, emits an odor extremely disgusting to human beings; it is even said that some persons have fainted after smelling it. A smaller relative, the black calla lily, which is also pollinated by beetles, smells like dead fish. The pollination process in these two plants is similar to that of the spotted arum lily.

You should not be left with the idea that all beetle flowers have unpleasant odors, however. The wine-like scent of *Calycanthus* is quite delightful, and many water lilies and magnolias emit pleasant odors.

Mosquitoes might seem to be too small and fragile to be good pollinators, but the *Habenaria* orchid, which grows in bogs and woods in the northern parts of North America, Europe, and Asia, is pollinated by mosquitoes, as well as by a few small moths. Anyone who has spent the summer months in Alaska or northern Canada knows how abundant mosquitoes can be in such areas. While a mosquito sips nectar from the spur of a tiny *Habenaria* flower, pollinia become attached to its eyes. When the mosquito visits the next flower, only a little bit of a pollinium breaks off onto the stigma, and the rest may come off on other flowers that the mosquito visits. In this way, many flowers can be pollinated by the pollinia from just one flower.

Perhaps you have noticed that all the pollinators we have discussed so far can fly. A flying animal can move more or less directly through the air from a flower on one plant to a flower on another, but a walking or crawling animal, especially a small one, ordinarily would have difficulty in bringing about the cross-pollination of most kinds of plants. Even if two apple trees are side by side, an ant is not likely to walk up the trunk of one tree, visit a few flowers, go down the trunk, cross the ground to the other tree, climb its trunk, and visit the flowers there. A bee or other flying insect can do the job much more efficiently.

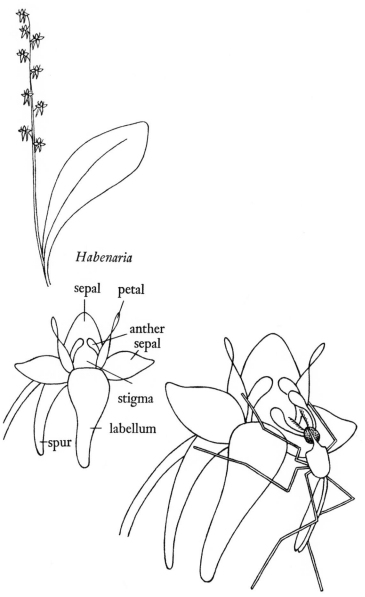

Habenaria

sepal petal

anther
sepal

stigma

spur labellum

MOSQUITO ON *Habenaria* FLOWER

Yet there are a few flowers pollinated by ants. One of these is a species of small knotweed that grows in the dry areas of Oregon. Its tiny flowers contain just enough nectar to attract ants but not larger pollinators, and its pollen is so sticky that it clings even to the smooth surfaces of ants. The plants are small and grow in dense clumps; this makes it easy for the ants to travel from plant to plant.

ANT ON KNOTWEED

· Pollination ·
by Birds

You might think that birds, with their covering of feathers on which pollen could so easily be caught, would be good pollinators, but very few birds visit flowers. Most pollinating birds are confined to the warmer parts of Asia, Africa, Australia, and New Zealand. Europe has none. Hummingbirds are the only pollinating birds throughout much of the United States, but if you live in the southwestern deserts, perhaps you have seen white-winged doves visiting the flowers of the giant saguaro cactus, which is pollinated by bats, too.

Birds are active by day and have a keen sense of sight. Their flowers are usually brightly colored, often red or orange. Some examples are: cardinal flower, scarlet sage (red salvia), fuchsia, trumpet vine, hibiscus, and bird-of-paradise. Bird-pollinated species of columbine and larkspur are red; those species with flowers of other colors are pollinated by insects. Some tropical bird flowers have vivid combinations of red, yellow, and green, called "parrot colors."

Birds have a poor sense of smell, and their flowers produce little or no odor.

Collecting nectar, which bird flowers usually produce in abundance, is the main reason birds visit flowers. The flowers usually are tubular in shape, and the birds insert their long tongues into the corolla to reach the nectar. Some of the birds have long beaks that match the shapes of their tongues.

Hummingbirds hover when they feed on nectar, and their flowers, like moth flowers, lack perches. Compare the flowers of two closely related plants: cardinal flower, which is bird-pollinated, and blue lobelia (page 33), which is pollinated by bumblebees. Each has a lower lip of three petals. In the blue

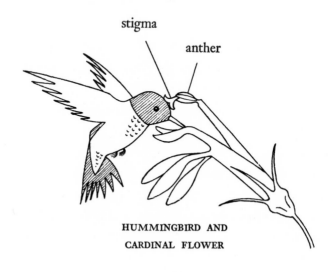

stigma

anther

HUMMINGBIRD AND
CARDINAL FLOWER

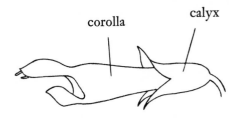

corolla   calyx

ANTHERS SHEDDING POLLEN

STIGMAS RECEPTIVE

SCARLET SAGE AND HUMMINGBIRD

lobelia this lip slants forward, and a bee can use it as a landing platform. In the cardinal flower, the lip hangs downward and provides no support to the hummingbirds. In both flowers the stamens and styles stand where they strike the head or back of the visitor.

Scarlet sage and blue meadow sage (page 64) are another such pair of closely related flowers. But there is only a small lower lip in the scarlet sage flower, whereas the bee-pollinated blue meadow sage has a large one. Both flowers have the same unusual anthers, but in scarlet sage they do not tilt on their filaments. In the close quarters of this flower, a hummingbird can hardly help bumping its head against the fertile half of the anther while taking nectar from deep in the corolla.

In poinsettia, it is the bright red bracts (modified leaves) that attract birds. The tiny flowers, so insignificant in appearance, are enclosed in little green cups. A small gland on the side of each cup holds nectar.

Birds are much stronger than insects, and they could do a great deal of damage to flowers lacking

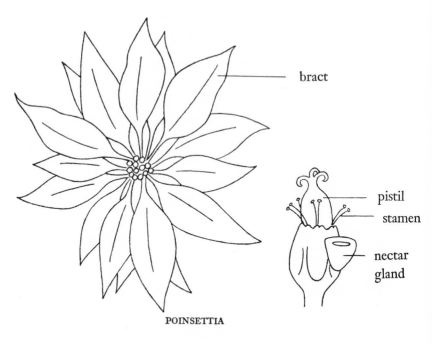

bract

pistil
stamen

nectar
gland

POINSETTIA

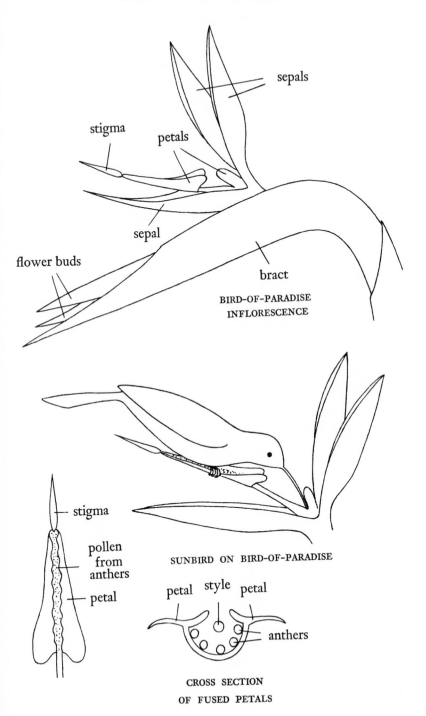

sepals

stigma

petals

sepal

flower buds

bract

**BIRD-OF-PARADISE
INFLORESCENCE**

SUNBIRD ON BIRD-OF-PARADISE

stigma

pollen
from
anthers

petal

petal   style   petal

anthers

**CROSS SECTION
OF FUSED PETALS**

some kind of protection against accidental pecks. The ovaries, in which the seeds develop, especially need protection. In most bird flowers, the ovaries are situated in a part of the flower in which the bird has no interest. The nectar-containing spurs of columbine, larkspur, and jewelweed direct the birds' beaks away from the ovaries. Some bird flowers are epigynous, with the ovary below the rest of the flower where it is not so likely to be pierced by a beak. In addition to being epigynous, fuchsia flowers hang loosely from their stems. If a bird pecks too vigorously at the flower, it merely swings away from the bird.

Bird-of-paradise flowers are native to South Africa, where they are pollinated by sunbirds. The plants are often grown in greenhouses, and you can find them in florists' shops. Each inflorescence consists of a few epigynous flowers with their ovaries surrounded by a single, large, reddish-purple bract. Usually one or two flowers are open at a time. Each flower has three orange sepals and three blue petals. One petal, which is small, conceals the nectar. The other two are united and form a single arrow-shaped structure with a groove down the middle. The stamens and style are hidden in the groove. When a sunbird seeking nectar rests on the lobes of the arrow, they spread apart. The exposed stamens then touch the underside of the bird and spread pollen on it. The stigma receives pollen when a bird, already dusted with pollen, touches it briefly before it lands on the petals.

· Pollination ·
by Bats

Viewing too many horror movies gives one the impression that all bats are vampire bats that feed on the blood of animal victims—including human beings. Actually there are many bats that feed peaceably on fruits and on the pollen and nectar of flowers. Being mammals, bats are covered with fur. This gives them a rough surface to which pollen grains can stick.

Bats, the only flying mammals, are active mostly at night, and their flowers open mostly at night. Bats are totally color-blind, and their flowers have either pale or drab colors. The flowers attract bats by emitting strong scents, which are described as stale or mousy. Bats are relatively large, active animals that require a great deal of food, and bat flowers usually produce great quantities of nectar, pollen, or both.

Insect-eating bats find their way easily in the dark

and avoid hitting even very small obstacles, but in bats that feed on plants this ability is poorly developed. Bat flowers stand well out from the leaves and stems of the plant, and this reduces the chances of a bat's becoming entangled in the branches in the dark. The flowers of the sausage tree of Africa are suspended on long, ropelike branches that hang straight down from sturdier branches. (The tree gets its name

BATS AT SAGUARO CACTUS

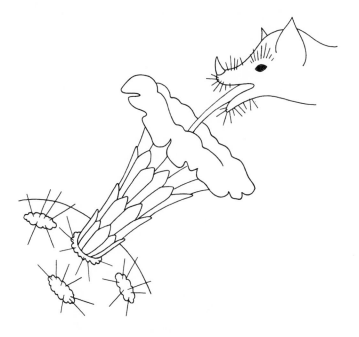

from the fact that its fruits look like sausages hanging on strings.) Some bananas are pollinated by bats.

Pollination by bats is most common in the tropics, but the century plant and some cactuses, including the giant saguaro of the American Southwest, have bat flowers.

· Pollination ·
by Water

Very few plants are pollinated by water. In fact, water usually is harmful to pollen grains, and most flowers are so constructed that the pollen rarely, if ever, gets wet. In closed flowers and in flowers that hang upside down and have short stamens, the corolla protects the anthers from rain. Anthers of many other plants open only in dry weather. Nearly all flowering plants that grow in water hold their flowers well above water level where the pollen grains may be transported by wind or animals.

In the Faroe Islands in the North Atlantic Ocean, the cool, rainy weather is poor for pollination by either wind or insects, and many species growing there are self-pollinated. But buttercups on these islands are among the few plants known to be pollinated by rain. Even a rainstorm three hours long does

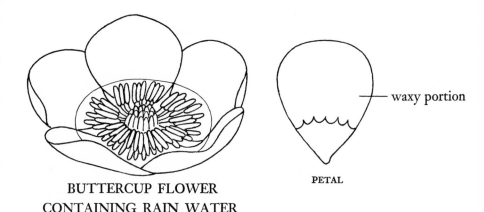

BUTTERCUP FLOWER
CONTAINING RAIN WATER

PETAL

waxy portion

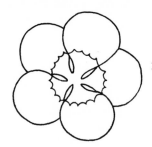

FLOWER WITH STAMENS AND
PISTILS REMOVED TO SHOW
DRAINAGE SPACES BETWEEN
THE PETALS

not harm their pollen. The five yellow petals of these buttercups curve upward in such a way that together they form a cup. Because the petals are very narrow at their bases, there are five small spaces between them near the bottom of the cup, and so the cup leaks as it begins to fill with water in a rainstorm. The outer part of each petal, the part near the rim of the cup, has a shiny, waxy surface that repels water. (You can see the same kind of thing happen if you spill a little water on a freshly waxed wooden surface. The water does not spread out as it would on unprotected wood; instead it rounds up in little beads that touch as little of the wax as possible.) The bases of the petals are not waxy and do not repel water. So even if more and more raindrops fall into a buttercup flower, the cup does not fill all the way. Instead it fills up to the waxy part of the petals, and the excess water leaks out from the bottom.

In a rainstorm, the flower holds just enough water to cover the stamens and pistils in the center of the flower, but not enough to overflow. Because pollen grains from open anthers float on the water surface, they are not lost by leaking through the bottom of the cup. Neither are they lost over the edge of the cup, because the water does not overflow. As the water swirls among the stamens and pistils, the flower is self-pollinated. In addition, some raindrops land in a cup with sufficient force to splash some of the water out of one flower and into another one. In this way, buttercup flowers are cross-pollinated as well as self-pollinated by rain.

Near your home you may find buttercups with the same kind of flowers, and it is possible that they may be pollinated by raindrops as well as by insects. Marsh marigold flowers are pollinated both by insects and rain; but these flowers have no petals, and the yellow sepals form the cup.

Vallisneria, or tape grass, is a common aquarium plant. It is pollinated in part by water and in part by wind, but in such a way that the pollen stays dry. These dioecious plants grow under water. A pistillate

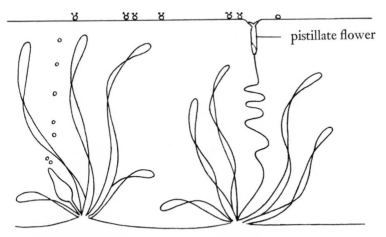

pistillate flower

STAMINATE PLANT
SHEDDING FLOWERS

PISTILLATE PLANT

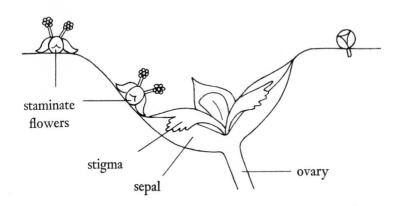

staminate
flowers

stigma

sepal

ovary

TAPE GRASS

flower bud forms at the tip of a short stem that grows upward until it reaches the surface of the water. Then the bud opens. As the flower rests on the water, it causes a slight depression to form on the surface of the water. The flower has three big sepals, three tiny petals, and a pistil with three large stigmas with fringed edges.

The staminate flower buds are formed under water, too. They become detached and rise to the surface. There they open and float like tiny boats. The sepals bend back so far that the two stamens are held above the water surface, where they stay dry. As the wind pushes the staminate flowers about on the water, at least a few of them are likely to float near a female flower. When a staminate flower nears the depression around the pistillate flower, it slides down the water surface and into the space between two of the sepals of the pistillate flower. As it slides down, the staminate flower tilts a little, and this causes one of its anthers to touch the fringed edge of the stigma and some of the pollen brushes off onto it. After pollination, the stem of the pistillate flower twists into a coil that draws the flower below the water where the seeds and fruits develop.

Eelgrasses, which grow along many ocean coastlines, are among the very few plants in which pollen actually travels *through* water. As in the case of wind dissemination, the chances of any pollen grain swirling about in the tides ever meeting the stigma of another eelgrass plant, are very low. The stigmas, like those of wind-pollinated flowers, stand well out from the flowers, but it is the pollen that has an interesting adaptation to water pollination. Unlike other pollen grains, which are spherical or nearly so, those of eelgrass (page 10) are long and threadlike. When they touch another object, they curl around it, attaching themselves securely to it. If that object happens to be an eelgrass stigma, pollination is accomplished.

· Energy and ·
Pollination

Why do we eat food? The first answer you might think of is to keep from being hungry. This is true, but eating does more for us. One thing it does is to supply us with the energy that our bodies need to stay alive, to grow, to move, and to do anything else we do, including obtaining more food. If you were a farmer and raised all your own food, you would have to raise enough to replace all the energy your body used in working in the fields to get that food, plus the energy you used in your spare-time activities. If you do not eat food containing enough energy to replace all the energy your body uses, then you begin to lose weight. If this were to continue for a long time, you would starve to death.

The same is true of animals. A butterfly that lives on the sugar (which contains energy) in the nectar it sips from flowers, must get at least enough energy from that nectar to replace all the energy it uses up in flying from flower to flower in search of nectar. It also needs additional energy for its other activities, such as finding a mate, laying eggs, or escaping from enemies.

Now let us look at this from another point of view—that of the plant being pollinated. What we have to say here pertains only to plants pollinated by animals seeking food in flowers; it does not pertain to plants pollinated by animals that come for other reasons and get their food elsewhere. If a plant is to be successfully pollinated, it must provide enough nectar to supply the energy needs of its pollinators. If the plant does not produce sufficient nectar to do that, then its pollinators will stop coming—either because they have starved to death or found other sources of nectar. Different pollinators have different energy requirements, and different species of plants produce quantities of nectar that correspond to these requirements.

The flowers of the little Oregon knotweed pollinated by ants (page 104) produce very little nectar. Because ants walk and run but do not fly, they need much less energy than most other pollinators, and so they can get along with what the knotweed flowers produce.

Active, flying insects, like bees, butterflies, and moths, use up much more energy than do ants, and their plants produce more nectar than does the knotweed. In those species with large flowers, like squash or columbine, each flower produces a great deal of nectar. Species with small flowers, such as the clovers or sunflowers, usually have the flowers clustered in dense inflorescences. Then, even though each flower produces only a small quantity of nectar, the insect can take a little from each flower in bloom and so get more food for each visit.

Bats and birds require even more energy than do most insects, not only because they are larger, but because they maintain a constant body temperature. Each species of mammal (of which you and bats are examples) and bird has its own natural body temperature. Keeping the body warm on a cold day or cool on a hot day requires energy. For this reason, bird and bat flowers must provide large quantities of nectar. It is not likely that animals much larger than bats or small birds would be regular pollinators, for their energy requirements would be too large to be supplied by flowers. Even those that do pollinate flowers usually get some of their food elsewhere.

Because birds and mammals (the so-called "warm-blooded" animals) maintain a constant body temperature, they can continue to be active in cold weather. Other animals (sometimes called "cold-blooded"), which include the insects, have no one constant normal body temperature; their temperatures usually go up and down as the weather changes. In cold weather they become cold and sluggish and visit few flowers, if any. In mountainous areas in the tropics, the higher you go, the fewer insect pollinators, and the more bird and bat pollinators, you find. In the Andes Mountains, bats have been observed pollinating flowers at altitudes of 10,000 feet where the temperature sometimes drops to freezing at night.

We should point out that even some cold-blooded animals can keep their bodies warm for some time in cool weather. Bumblebees "warm up" their flight muscles by contracting and relaxing them quickly and repeatedly before flying. Even on a frosty morning bumblebees may be visiting flowers when other insects are still inactive. Of course, this warming-up requires extra energy, too.

Although a plant must provide enough nectar to supply its pollinators' needs, producing too much nectar can reduce the efficiency of pollination. If a visiting pollinator finds a great deal of nectar at one flower, it will not need to seek out many more flowers to get all it needs. The fewer flowers it visits, the less cross-pollination it accomplishes. The best arrangement for a plant seems to be to produce just a little more nectar than its pollinators need, and to have its flowers so constructed or so guarded as to prevent smaller robbers from reaching the nectar. Larger robbers probably will not come often for they will not find enough nectar for their needs.

Robbers are not always bad for pollination, however. In fact, they sometimes increase the amount of cross-pollination. Red clover, for instance, is pollinated by long-tongued bumblebees and honeybees, which pollinate the flowers as they insert their tongues from the front of the·keel. Short-tongued bumblebees, which cannot reach the nectar from the front, sometimes bite holes in the side of the keel and steal nectar through the holes. In one study, it was found that short-tongued bumblebees taking a little nectar from red clover flowers actually increased the quantity of seed produced by the plants. When the robbers were present, long-tongued bumblebees were forced to visit more red clover plants to get enough nectar for their needs than they would have if the robbers had not been there.

· A Summer ·
Project

If you have a sunny garden space available to you,
you might like to plant a small garden and observe
the pollination of different species as they come into
bloom. Several of the species mentioned in this book
are common garden plants, and you can buy either
seeds or young plants in garden shops. Some sugges-
tions are: snapdragon, pea, green bean, everlasting
pea, zucchini squash, blue meadow sage (or blue salvia, which is similar), sunflower, primrose, pansy,
phlox, columbine, scarlet sage (red salvia), corn,
tomato.

You probably won't have room to plant all of
these. Also, a few may not be available in your area
if the climate is not suitable for them.

After making your selections, plan your garden so
that the tallest plants are in the northern part of the

garden and the shortest to the south. This way, the tall plants will not shade the small ones. All of these plants do best with plenty of sun. Sunflowers and corn will be tall. Pole beans, most peas, and tomatoes grow tall if provided with stakes for support. Zucchini squash is a little smaller. Snapdragons, columbines, and scarlet sage are medium-sized. Phlox and primrose exist in varieties of different sizes. Dwarf varieties of peas and beans grow only about a foot high. Pansies are small plants. Follow the directions on the seed packages so that you do not crowd the plants or plant the seeds too deep.

When the plants are in bloom, try to observe pollination. Remove a few flowers to examine them more closely.

Allow some flowers to remain on the plants to see if they set seed. If you have only a few corn plants, natural pollination probably will be poor, because the wind will blow most of the pollen away from the plants. You could remove a staminate inflorescence (the tassel) when it is shedding pollen and shake it directly over the silks, or even rub it against the silks.

If you don't have a garden but do have a small sunny space, you might grow a few of the smaller plants in flowerpots. Potted corn and sunflowers will not do well unless they are in very large flowerpots, and these can be quite expensive. You can make your own medium-sized flowerpots out of one-gallon plastic containers like the kind in which distilled water is sold. With a scissors, remove the top half of the container. Make your cut just under the handle. Cut a few small holes in the bottom for drainage. For a tray, use any old plate—the aluminum plate from a frozen pie will do well. Corn and sunflower plants probably will not reach full height this way, but you should be able to see the flower parts when they form.

Potted plants must be watered frequently, especially in hot, dry weather. Check the soil every day. It should be damp, but not soaking wet.

If you do not have a good place in which to raise your own plants—and even if you do—you can find plants in bloom elsewhere: a friend's garden, a park, a botanical garden, an arboretum, a vacant lot in the city, or a roadside in the country. In most parks there are rules against picking flowers, but you should have opportunity to observe pollination. One nice thing about vacant lots is that usually no one cares if you pick a few flowers.

A friend will probably be glad to tell you the names of his plants. Some parks have nature trails with the names of at least a few plants indicated, or a naturalist may be on hand. Rarely is there anyone to identify plants in a vacant lot or along a roadside, and so the accompanying illustrations may help you a little. It shows some of the most widespread weeds in the United States. Your library probably has books on local weeds and wild flowers that will help you to identify other plants.

If you find a convenient spot you like, return to it every week or so. There will probably be several

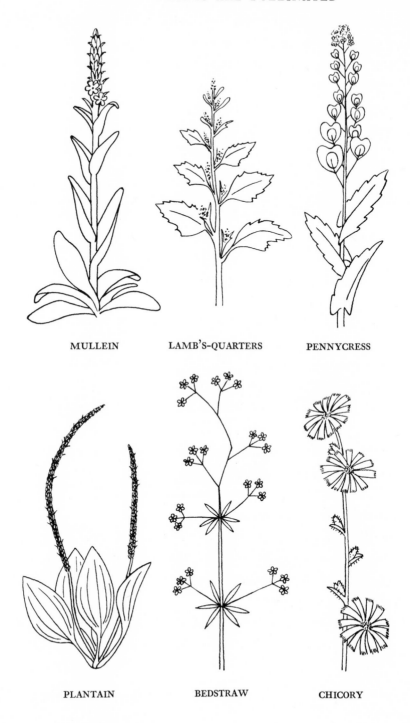

MULLEIN   LAMB'S-QUARTERS   PENNYCRESS

PLANTAIN   BEDSTRAW   CHICORY

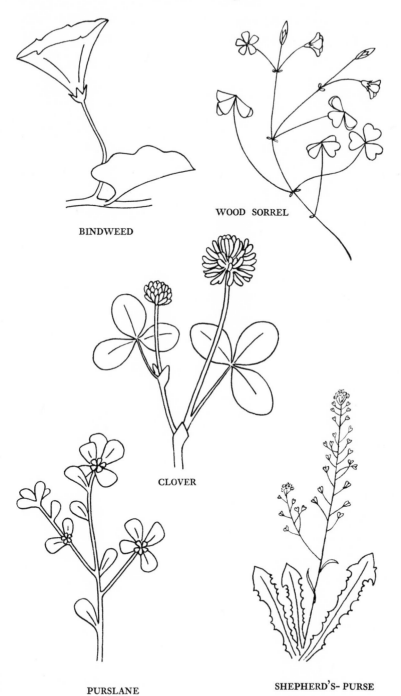

A SUMMER PROJECT

BINDWEED

WOOD SORREL

CLOVER

PURSLANE

SHEPHERD'S- PURSE

new species in bloom every time you go. How are the flowers pollinated? Can you tell if all the insects visiting flowers are pollinators or are some of them robbers?

If the spot is near your home, choose one warm, sunny day and visit it several times from early morning until sunset. Do you find the same flowers open at every visit, or are some flowers open at only certain times of day? Do you find the same insects at every visit or are some insects abroad at only certain times of day? Is there any connection between the two?

After studying pollination stories in many different kinds of plants, you will appreciate how living things depend on each other and on their physical environment.

· Glossary ·

anther: the upper part of a stamen; most anthers have two chambers called anther sacs in which pollen grains are produced

bract: a type of modified leaf; many bracts are immediately below a flower and may resemble sepals

calyx: all the sepals of a flower

central cell: a cell in the embryo sac of an ovule; if the central cell is fertilized by a sperm cell it develops into endosperm

column: the fused stamens, style, and stigma of an orchid flower

corolla: all the petals of a flower

cross-pollination: pollination of the stigma of a flower by pollen from another plant

dioecious: referring to plants that have staminate and pistillate flowers on different plants *egg cell:* a cell in the embryo sac of an ovule; if the egg cell is fertilized by a sperm cell it develops into an embryo

embryo: a young plant inside an ovule or seed; an embryo forms only after the egg cell in an ovule is fertilized by a sperm cell from a pollen tube

embryo sac: the portion of an ovule that before fertilization contains an egg cell and a central cell and that after fertilization contains the developing embryo and endosperm

endosperm: a food-storing tissue in some seeds; endosperm forms after the central cell in an ovule is fertilized by a sperm cell; in some species the endosperm disintegrates early, but in others it remains in the seed and is used up only after the seed germinates

epigynous: referring to a flower in which the sepals, petals, and stamens appear to arise from the top of the ovary

fertilization: in flowering plants, the fusion of a sperm cell with an egg cell or a central cell in an ovule

filament: the stalk of a stamen

generative cell: one of the cells of a pollen grain; the generative cell divides into two sperm cells

hermaphroditic: having both stamens and pistils in the same flower

hypogynous: referring to a flower in which the sepals, petals, and stamens appear to arise from below the ovary

inflorescence: a cluster of flowers more or less closely grouped on a stem

labellum: the large, conspicuous petal of an orchid flower *monoecious:* referring to plants that have staminate and pistillate flowers on the same plant

nectar: a sugary solution secreted by some flowers; nectar is used as a food by some animals and attracts them to flowers ready for pollination

nectar guide: a set of marks on a flower that indicate the location of nectar; nectar-seeking animals may learn to recognize these marks

ovary: the lower part of a pistil; the ovary contains one or more ovules that may ripen into seeds after pollination

ovule: the portion of an ovary that ripens into a seed if the egg cell and central cell within it are fertilized by sperm cells from a pollen grain; there may be one or more ovules in an ovary

perianth: all the sepals and petals (or all the tepals) of a flower

perigynous: referring to a flower in which the sepals, petals, and stamens appear to arise from the rim of a cup surrounding the ovary

petals: one of the flat organs between the sepals and stamens of a flower (or between the sepals and pistils, if the flower lacks stamens); petals usually are some color other than green

pistil: the female part of a flower; it usually consists of an ovary, one or more styles, and one or more stigmas

pistillate: referring to flowers that have pistils but no stamens; also referring to inflorescences or plants that have only pistillate flowers

pollen: a collective term for pollen grains

pollen basket: a special set of hairs on the hind legs of

bees; while on collecting trips bees store pollen grains temporarily in their pollen baskets

pollen grain: one of many fine grains produced in an anther; after arriving on the stigma of a pistil, the pollen grain produces a pollen tube containing two sperm cells and a tube cell

pollen tube: a tube that develops from a pollen grain after the pollen grain lands on a receptive stigma; the pollen tube grows down through the pistil toward an ovule

pollination: the transfer of pollen grains from an anther to a stigma

pollinium: a sac of pollen grains; only a few plants, orchids and milkweeds, for example, produce pollen grains in pollinia; usually the entire pollinium is transferred to a stigma

robber: an animal that takes nectar from a flower without bringing about pollination

seed: a ripened ovule; it contains an embryo and, in some species, endosperm

self-pollination: pollination of the stigma of a flower by pollen from the same flower or from another flower on the same plant

sepal: one of the flat, leaflike, usually green parts of a flower; sepals are below the petals (or to the outside if the flower bud has not yet opened)

spadix: an inflorescence consisting of many tiny flowers crowded on a stem surrounded by a special bract called a spathe

spathe: a bract associated with a spadix

sperm cells: two cells produced by the division of the generative cell in a pollen tube; fertilization of an egg cell by a sperm cell is necessary for the development of an embryo, and fertilization of a central cell is necessary for the development of endosperm

spur: a nectar-containing sac on a petal or sepal

stamen: the male part of a flower; it consists of a stalk called a filament and an anther in which pollen grains are produced

staminate: referring to flowers that have stamens but no pistils; also referring to inflorescences or plants that have only staminate flowers

stigma: the portion of a pistil that is receptive to pollen grains; the stigma usually is at the tip of a style, but in pistils lacking styles it is directly on the ovary

style: a stalk extending above an ovary; a style bears one or more stigmas

tepal: a perianth part that cannot be identified as either a sepal or a petal

tube cell: one of the cells of a pollen grain; it precedes the sperm cells down the pollen tube